Introduction

Did you know that everything tastes better on a stick? Yes, a stick can serve a practical purpose when eating a cake ball or cookie, but it also turns them into pops—the creative, cute, fun and slightly mad treats that will add a little humour to your day.

Make Me Cake and Cookie Pops will introduce you to this baking and confectionery phenomenon. From dead-easy pops made from marshmallows that are perfect for children to make, through to the more challenging projects such as mini gingerbread houses decorated with lollies and snow-white icing, within these pages you will find more than 50 creative ideas.

These pops will take you to an ocean world with jewelled fish, transport you to a wintry day with shimmering snowflakes, invite you to the fair with caramel popcorn on sticks and send you out to the countryside with the cutest animals around. There are robots for boys, flowers for girls, brownies, sports balls, Christmas puddings, spider webs and rocky road pops—this book will inspire creativity and make you, and your loved ones, smile.

Towards the end of the book you will find the basics chapter filled with standard recipes to form the base of your pops, and loads of helpful hints and tips for making pops—an invaluable resource for both beginners and more experienced 'pop makers'. And remember, a stick not only makes something taste better, it also makes it more fun!

make me

cake and cookie pops

Contents

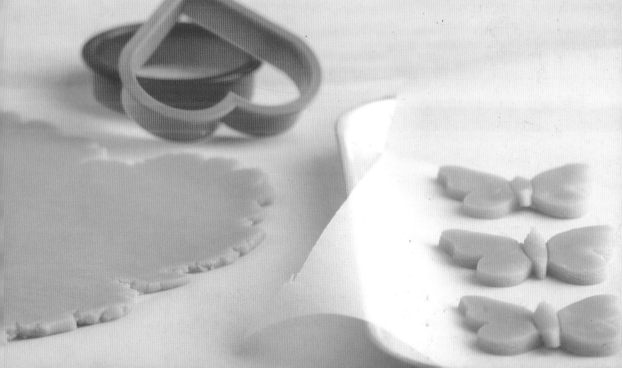

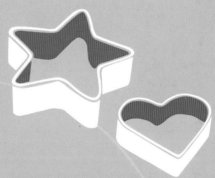

Cookie pops

Polka dot cookie pops

Preparation time: 30 minutes (+ 30 minutes chilling time, cooling time and 2 hours standing time)
Cooking time: 15 minutes (per batch)
Makes: about 20

125 g (4½ oz) unsalted butter, cubed, just softened
110 g (3¾ oz/½ cup) caster (superfine) sugar
1 egg, at room temperature
¼ teaspoon vanilla extract
150 g (5½ oz/1 cup) plain (all-purpose) flour
150 g (5½ oz/1 cup) self-raising flour
Smarties, to decorate
1 quantity royal icing (see page 124)
20 paddle pop sticks, coloured, if desired
(see page 120)

TIP: Keep pops in an airtight container in a cool place for up to 1 week.

1 Preheat oven to 160°C (315°F/Gas 2–3). Line three large baking trays with non-stick baking paper.

2 Use an electric mixer to beat the butter and sugar in a medium bowl until pale and creamy. Add the egg and vanilla and beat until well combined. Sift together the flours, add to the butter mixture and mix on low speed until just combined and a soft dough forms.

3 Divide the biscuit dough into two even portions and shape each into a disc. Roll out each portion evenly between two sheets of non-stick baking paper until 5 mm (¼ in) thick. Place the dough on two of the baking trays and refrigerate for 30 minutes or until firm.

4 Cut the dough into 20 squares using a 6 cm (2½ in) cutter or a sharp knife and place 3 cm (1¼ in) apart on the lined trays. Reroll and cut any scraps of dough if necessary. Press the Smarties into the biscuits to decorate.

5 Bake the biscuits, in batches if necessary, for 15 minutes, swapping the trays halfway through cooking, or until lightly golden and cooked through. Allow to cool for 5 minutes on trays before transferring to a wire rack to cool completely.

6 Use some of the royal icing to attach a paddle pop stick to the back of each biscuit. Set aside for 2 hours or until the icing sets and the paddle pop sticks are firmly attached.

Almond macaron pops

Preparation time: 30 minutes (+ 1 hour 30 minutes standing
 time and cooling time)
Cooking time: 25–28 minutes
Makes: 15

215 g (7½ oz/1¾ cups) icing
  (confectioners') sugar
125 g (4½ oz/1¼ cups) almond meal
3 egg whites, at room temperature
pinch of salt
55 g (2 oz/¼ cup) caster (superfine) sugar
½ teaspoon vanilla essence
food colouring of your choice
150 g (5½ oz) white chocolate,
  melted, cooled
15 paddle pop sticks

TIPS: Keep pops in an
airtight container in the
fridge for up to 3 days.

You can use these pops
to decorate a Christening
cake or as party favours
wrapped in cellophane bags
and tied with ribbons.

1 Preheat oven to 140°C (275°F/Gas 1). Line two large baking trays with non-stick baking paper.
Use a 4 cm (1½ in) round cutter to mark 30 circles on the paper then turn the paper over.
2 Put the icing sugar and almond meal in the bowl of a food processor. Process until
well combined.
3 Use an electric mixer with a whisk attachment to whisk the egg whites and salt in a clean, dry
medium bowl until soft peaks form. Gradually add the caster sugar, a spoonful at a time, whisking
well after each addition until firm peaks form. Whisk in the vanilla. Sprinkle half the almond
mixture over the egg whites and use a large metal spoon or spatula to fold in gently.
Fold in the remaining almond mixture. Fold in enough food colouring to tint to desired colour.
4 Use a large piping (icing) bag fitted with a 1 cm (½ in) plain nozzle to pipe the mixture onto
the trays to fill the circles, holding the piping nozzle directly above the marked circles. Set aside
for 30 minutes.
5 Bake the macarons for 25–28 minutes, swapping the trays halfway through cooking, or until
the macarons feel firm to the touch and are cooked underneath. Allow to cool for 5 minutes
on trays before transferring to a wire rack to cool completely.
6 Spread a small teaspoon of the melted chocolate onto one macaron. Place a paddle pop
stick on the chocolate and top with another ¼ teaspoon of chocolate. Sandwich with another
macaron. Repeat with the remaining macarons, chocolate and paddle pop sticks. Set aside for
1 hour or until the chocolate sets and the paddle pop sticks are firmly attached.

Alphabet cookie pops

Preparation time: 20 minutes (+ 30 minutes chilling and 2 hours standing time)
Cooking time: 20 minutes
Decorating time: 30 minutes
Makes: 35

> 1 quantity vanilla biscuit dough (see page 116)
> 2 quantities glacé icing (see page 120)
> food colourings of your choice
> 35 x 20 cm (8 in) thick wooden skewers or
>   paddle pop sticks, coloured, if desired (see page 120)
> sprinkles, to decorate

1 Preheat oven to 160°C (315°F/Gas 2–3). Line two large baking trays with non-stick baking paper.

2 Divide the biscuit dough into two even portions. Roll out each portion evenly between two sheets of non-stick baking paper until 7 mm (⅜ in) thick. Place the dough on the baking trays and refrigerate for 30 minutes or until firm.

3 Cut the dough into 35 shapes using alphabet cutters and place 2 cm (¾ in) apart on the lined trays. Reroll and cut any scraps of dough if necessary.

4 Bake the biscuits for 20 minutes, swapping the trays halfway through cooking, or until lightly golden and cooked through. Allow to cool for 5 minutes on trays before transferring to a wire rack to cool completely.

5 To decorate, tint the glacé icing with the food colouring to desired colours. Use a palette knife that has been dipped in hot water to spread the icing over the biscuits. Sprinkle some of the biscuits with the sprinkles to decorate. Set aside for 30 minutes or until the icing sets.

6 Use some of the remaining icing to attach a skewer or paddle pop stick to the back of each biscuit. Set aside for 2 hours or until the icing sets and the skewers are firmly attached.

TIP: Keep pops in an airtight container in a cool place for up to 1 week.

Chocolate meringue kiss pops

Preparation time: 30 minutes (+ 1 hour cooling and 40 minutes standing time)
Cooking time: 30 minutes
Makes: 20

2 egg whites, at room temperature
110 g (3¾ oz/½ cup) caster (superfine) sugar
¼ teaspoon ground cinnamon
20 lollipop sticks

Filling
125 g (4½ oz) dark chocolate, chopped
85 g (3 oz/⅓ cup) sour cream

1 Preheat oven to 120°C (235°F/Gas ½). Line two large baking trays with non-stick baking paper.
2 Use an electric mixer with a whisk attachment to whisk the egg whites in a clean, dry, medium bowl until soft peaks form. Gradually add the sugar, a spoonful at a time, whisking well after each addition, until the sugar dissolves and the mixture is thick and glossy. Whisk in the cinnamon until evenly combined.
3 Use a piping (icing) bag fitted with a 1 cm (½ in) star nozzle to pipe the mixture into 40 x 3 cm (1¼ in) diameter stars on the lined trays, 3 cm apart. Bake the meringues for 30 minutes, swapping the trays halfway through cooking, or until crisp. Turn the oven off and cool with the door ajar for 1 hour or until cool to touch.
4 To make the filling, put the chocolate and sour cream in a small heatproof bowl over a saucepan of simmering water, making sure the base of the bowl doesn't touch the water. Stir until the chocolate melts and the mixture is smooth. Remove from the heat and cool for 10 minutes or until thick. Sandwich the meringues together with the filling, placing a lollipop stick in the middle. Set aside for 30 minutes or until the filling is firm.

TIP: Keep unfilled meringues in an airtight container in a cool place for up to 1 week. Sandwich them on the day of serving.

Traffic light cookie pops

Preparation time: 30 minutes (+ 30 minutes chilling time)
Cooking time: 25 minutes
Makes: 18

1 quantity vanilla biscuit dough (see page 116)
1½ tablespoons strawberry jam
3 tablespoons apricot jam
green food colouring
18 paddle pop sticks, coloured, if desired (see page 120)

1 Preheat oven to 160°C (315°F/Gas 2–3). Line two large baking trays with non-stick baking paper.
2 Divide the biscuit dough into two even portions. Roll out each portion evenly between two sheets of non-stick baking paper to a rectangle 36 x 16 cm (14¼ x 6¼ in) and 3 mm (⅛ in) thick. Place the dough on the baking trays and refrigerate for 30 minutes or until firm.
3 Use a ruler as a guide to cut out 36 rectangles, each measuring 4 x 8 cm (1½ x 3¼ in). Place 18 of the rectangles on the trays 2 cm (¾ in) apart, and place a paddle pop stick on each, extending one-third up the biscuit. Use a round 2 cm (¾ in) cutter to cut three evenly spaced holes from the remaining 18 rectangles. Sandwich the cookies with the holes on top of the biscuits on the tray. If necessary, trim the edges of the biscuits to neaten.
4 Stir the strawberry jam in a small bowl until smooth. Divide the apricot jam between two bowls. Tint one of the apricot jam portions with the green food colouring to desired colour. Stir both until smooth. Put small amounts of red, yellow and green jam (to resemble traffic lights) into the holes in the biscuits.
5 Bake the biscuits for 25 minutes, swapping the trays halfway through cooking, or until lightly golden and cooked through. Allow to cool for 5 minutes on trays before transferring to a wire rack to cool completely.

TIP: Keep pops in an airtight container in a cool place for up to 4 days.

Viennese finger pops

Preparation time: 30 minutes (+ cooling time and 1 hour standing time)
Cooking time: 15 minutes
Decorating time: 10 minutes
Makes: 12–14

100 g (3½ oz) unsalted butter, just softened
40 g (1½ oz/⅓ cup) icing (confectioners') sugar, sifted
1½ teaspoons vanilla extract
2 egg yolks, lightly whisked
150 g (5½ oz/1 cup) plain (all-purpose) flour, sifted
130 g (4½ oz) dark chocolate, chopped
40 g (1½ oz) unsalted butter, extra
12–14 short, flat wooden spoons

1 Preheat oven to 180°C (350°F/Gas 4). Line two large baking trays with non-stick baking paper. Use an electric mixer to beat the butter, icing sugar and vanilla in a small bowl until pale and creamy. Gradually add the egg yolk and beat thoroughly. Transfer to a large bowl, add the flour, and mix with a wooden spoon until just combined and the mixture is smooth.

2 Use a piping (icing) bag fitted with a 1 cm (½ in) star nozzle to pipe the mixture into 12–14 x 6 cm (2½ in) wavy lengths on the lined trays (see tip), about 3 cm (1¼ in) apart.

3 Bake the biscuits for 15 minutes, swapping the trays halfway through cooking, or until lightly golden and cooked through. Allow to cool for 5 minutes on trays before transferring to a wire rack to cool completely.

4 Line one of the trays with a new piece of non-stick baking paper. Place the chocolate and extra butter in a small heatproof bowl over a saucepan of simmering water, making sure the base of the bowl doesn't touch the water. Stir until melted and smooth. Dip half of a biscuit into the melted chocolate mixture to coat and place on the lined tray on top of a flat wooden spoon. Repeat with the remaining biscuits, chocolate mixture and spoons. Set aside for 1 hour or until the chocolate sets and the sticks are firmly attached.

TIPS: Keep pops in an airtight container in a cool place for up to 4 days.

To make piping easier, fold down the bag by 5 cm (2 in) before spooning the mixture in, then unfold. The top will be clean and easy to twist, thereby stopping the mixture from squirting out the top.

Flower cookie pops

Preparation time: 30 minutes (+ 30 minutes chilling
 and 2 hours standing time)
Cooking time: 15 minutes
Decorating time: 30 minutes
Makes: 12

120 g (4¼ oz) fondant icing
cornflour (cornstarch), to dust
1 quantity vanilla biscuit dough (see page 116)
12 paddle pop sticks
2 quantities royal icing (see page 124)
blue and green food colouring
yellow and orange rainbow choc chips

TIP: Keep pops in an airtight container in a cool place for up to 3 days.

1 Line a tray with non-stick baking paper. Divide the fondant into two even portions. Lightly dust a bench and rolling pin with the cornflour and roll out each portion of fondant until 1 mm (1⁄32 in) thick. Cut the fondant into 60 shapes using a 2.5 cm (1 in) petal cutter. Arrange in a single layer on the lined tray. Set aside at room temperature for 1 hour or until firm.

2 Meanwhile, preheat oven to 180°C (350°F/Gas 4). Line two large baking trays with non-stick baking paper.

3 Divide the biscuit dough into two even portions. Roll out each portion evenly between two sheets of non-stick baking paper until 5 mm (¼ in) thick. Place the dough on the baking trays and refrigerate for 30 minutes or until firm.

4 Cut the dough into 12 shapes using an 8.5 cm (3¼ in) round cutter and place 2 cm (¾ in) apart on the lined trays. Reroll and cut any scraps of dough if necessary.

5 Bake the biscuits for 15 minutes, swapping the trays around halfway through cooking, or until lightly golden and cooked through. Allow to cool for 5 minutes on trays before transferring to a wire rack to cool completely.

6 Reserve 125 ml (4 fl oz/½ cup) of the royal icing, cover with plastic wrap and set aside. Halve the remaining royal icing and tint one portion with the blue food colouring to desired colour and the other portion green to desired colour. Use a small palette knife that has been dipped in hot water to spread six of the biscuits with the blue icing to coat. Arrange five petals on each biscuit to make a flower. Repeat with the remaining biscuits, green icing and petals. Sprinkle the centre of the blue biscuits with the yellow rainbow choc chips and the green biscuits with the orange rainbow choc chips. Use some of the reserved icing to attach a paddle pop stick to the back of each biscuit. Set aside for 2 hours or until the icing sets and the sticks are firmly attached.

Chocolate chip cookie pops

Preparation time: 25 minutes (+ cooling time and 30 minutes standing time)
Cooking time: 15–18 minutes
Makes: 20

250 g (9 oz) unsalted butter, just softened
220 g (7¾ oz/1 cup) caster (superfine) sugar
1 egg, at room temperature
1 teaspoon vanilla essence
335 g (11¾ oz/2¼ cups) plain (all-purpose) flour
250 g (9 oz) milk or dark chocolate, chopped
20 paddle pop sticks
300 g (10½ oz) milk chocolate, melted

1 Preheat oven to 180°C (350°F/Gas 4). Line two large baking trays with non-stick baking paper.
2 Use an electric mixer to beat the butter and sugar in a medium bowl until pale and creamy. Add the egg and vanilla and beat until well combined. Add the flour and chopped chocolate and mix on low speed until just combined.
3 Roll 2 tablespoons of the mixture into balls and press onto the top one-third of a paddle pop stick. Place 4 cm (1½ in) apart on the lined trays and then flatten the mixture slightly.
4 Bake the biscuits for 15–18 minutes, swapping the trays halfway through cooking, or until lightly golden and cooked through. Allow to cool for 5 minutes on trays before transferring to a wire rack to cool completely.
5 Use a palette knife to spread the melted chocolate over the underside of the biscuits. Set aside for 30 minutes or until set.

TIPS: Keep pops in an airtight container in a cool place for up to 5 days.

These are great kids' party treats.

Chocolate & vanilla spiral cookie pops

Preparation time: 25 minutes (+ 1 hour chilling time)
Cooking time: 18–20 minutes (per batch)
Makes: 40

> 1 quantity vanilla biscuit dough (see page 116)
> 1 quantity chocolate biscuit dough (see page 116)
> 40 paddle pop sticks

1 Divide each biscuit dough into two even portions. Roll out each portion evenly between two sheets of non-stick baking paper to a 35 x 25 cm (14 x 10 in) rectangle and 3 mm (⅛ in) thick.

2 Place the vanilla and chocolate dough rectangles on a flat surface and remove the top sheets of baking paper. Invert the two vanilla dough rectangles on top of the chocolate dough rectangles to cover and then remove the top piece of the baking paper. Trim the edges so the rectangles measure approximately 33 x 24 cm (13 x 9½ in). Starting at the long edge closest to you and using the baking paper still attached to the base of the chocolate dough, roll the dough firmly into a log to create a spiral effect—make sure you roll it as tightly and evenly as possible. Place the two rolls of biscuit dough on a baking tray lined with non-stick baking paper and refrigerate for 1 hour or until firm.

3 Preheat oven to 180°C (350°F/Gas 4). Line three large baking trays with non-stick baking paper.

4 Use a sharp knife to cut the dough into 1.2 cm (½ in) slices. Place on baking trays about 3 cm (1¼ in) apart and insert a paddle pop stick into each, extending halfway into the biscuit. Press down on the biscuit with the heel of your hand to flatten very slightly—this will help to reshape the biscuits.

5 Bake the biscuits, in batches if necessary, for 18–20 minutes, swapping the trays around after 10 minutes, or until lightly golden and cooked through. Cool on trays.

TIP: Keep pops in an airtight container in a cool place for up to 1 week.

Chocolate peppermint cream pops

Preparation time: 40 minutes (+ 30 minutes chilling time
and 1 hour 30 minutes standing time)
Cooking time: 10 minutes
Makes: 20

½ quantity chocolate biscuit dough (see page 116)
1 egg white
290 g (10¼ oz/2⅓ cups) pure icing (confectioners')
  sugar, sifted, plus extra, for kneading
2–3 drops peppermint extract, or to taste
20 lollipop sticks

Chocolate coating
200 g (7 oz) dark chocolate, chopped
200 g (7 oz) dark compound chocolate (see note page 122)

TIP: Keep pops in an
airtight container in a cool
place for up to 4 days.

1 Preheat oven to 180°C (350°F/Gas 4). Line two baking trays with non-stick baking paper.
2 Divide the biscuit dough into two even portions. Roll out each portion evenly between two
sheets of non-stick baking paper until 3 mm (⅛ in) thick. Place the dough on the baking trays
and refrigerate for 30 minutes or until firm.
3 Cut the dough into 20 rounds using a 4 cm (1½ in) cutter and place 2 cm (¾ in) apart
on the lined trays. Reroll and cut any scraps of dough if necessary. Bake the biscuits for
10 minutes, swapping the trays halfway through cooking, or until cooked through.
Allow to cool for 5 minutes on trays before transferring to a wire rack to cool completely.
4 To make the peppermint cream, put the egg white in a clean, dry, small bowl. Use an
electric mixer on low speed to beat in the icing sugar, 2 tablespoons at a time, until well
combined. Add more icing sugar, if necessary, until a soft dough forms. Turn the dough
onto a bench dusted with icing sugar. Add the peppermint extract and knead in enough
icing sugar so that the dough is not sticky.
5 Roll a teaspoonful of the peppermint cream into a ball and flatten to the size of the biscuits.
Sandwich with a lollipop stick between two chocolate biscuits, pressing together gently. Repeat
with the remaining filling, chocolate biscuits and sticks, keeping the filling covered as you work.
Set aside for 30 minutes or until the filling sets.
6 To make the coating, put the chopped chocolate and compound chocolate in a heatproof
bowl over a saucepan of simmering water, making sure the base of the bowl doesn't touch the
water. Stir until the chocolate melts. Remove from the heat and allow to cool slightly. Dip the
biscuits one at a time into the chocolate and then gently tap the stick on the edge of the bowl
to remove excess chocolate. Set aside on a lined tray for 1 hour or until set.

Lollipops

Preparation time: 30 minutes (+ 30 minutes chilling time)
Cooking time: 10–12 minutes
Makes: 16

1 quantity vanilla biscuit dough (see page 116)
300 g (10½ oz) assorted boiled lollies
16 paddle pop sticks

1 Preheat oven to 200°C (400°F/Gas 6). Line two large baking trays with non-stick baking paper.

2 Divide the biscuit dough into two even portions. Roll out each portion evenly between two sheets of non-stick baking paper until 5 mm (¼ in) thick. Place the dough on the baking trays and refrigerate for 30 minutes or until firm.

3 Separate the lollies into their different colours and use a rolling pin to crush finely.

4 Cut the dough into 16 rounds using an 8.5 cm (3¼ in) cutter and place 2 cm (¾ in) apart on the lined trays, leaving space for the sticks. Reroll and cut any scraps of dough if necessary. Use a 5.5 cm (2¼ in) round cutter to cut a circle inside the rounds and then a 2 cm (¾ in) cutter to cut a circle in the centre of each 5.5 cm round. Remove the biscuit dough between the 5.5 cm round and the 2 cm cutter and discard.

5 Slide a paddle pop stick under each to extend to the centre round.

6 Bake the biscuits for 5 minutes. Remove from the oven and fill each cut-out section of the biscuits with the crushed lollies. Return to the oven and bake the biscuits for another 5–7 minutes or until the lollies melt and the biscuits are golden brown and cooked through. Cool on trays.

TIP: Put pops in an airtight container once cooled or the cooked lollies will soften. Keep in a cool place for up to 2 days.

Monster cookie pops

Preparation time: 20 minutes (+ 30 minutes chilling time,
  cooling time and 2 hours standing time)
Cooking time: 10–12 minutes (per batch)
Decorating time: 20 minutes
Makes: 50

1 quantity chocolate or vanilla biscuit dough (see page 116)
2 quantities royal icing (see page 124)
food colouring of your choice
Smarties and/or mixed candy-coated chocolates, to decorate
50 paddle pop sticks, coloured, if desired (see page 120)

1 Preheat oven to 180°C (350°F/Gas 4). Line three large
baking trays with non-stick baking paper.
2 Divide the biscuit dough into two even portions. Roll out
each portion evenly between two sheets of non-stick baking
paper until 5 mm (¼ in) thick. Place the dough on two of the
baking trays and refrigerate for 30 minutes or until firm.
3 Cut the dough into 50 shapes using a 6.5 cm long x 4.5 cm
wide (2½ in x 1¾ in) small gingerbread man cutter and place
2 cm (¾ in) apart on the trays. Reroll and cut any scraps of
dough if necessary.
4 Bake the biscuits, in batches if necessary, for 10–12 minutes,
swapping the trays after 7 minutes, or until cooked through.
Allow to cool for 5 minutes on trays before transferring to a
wire rack to cool completely.
5 To decorate, set aside half of the royal icing for attaching
the sticks. Tint the remaining icing with the food colouring
to desired colour. Use a small piping (icing) bag fitted with
a 2 mm (¹⁄₁₆ in) nozzle to pipe a thin line around the edge of
the biscuits. (Alternatively, use a zip-lock bag with a small hole
cut in the corner.) Attach the Smarties and/or candy-coated
chocolates with a little icing as eyes. Use some of the reserved
icing to attach a paddle pop stick to the back of each biscuit.
Set aside for 2 hours or until the icing sets and the sticks are
firmly attached.

TIPS: Keep pops in an airtight container in a cool place for up to 1 week.

Use these to decorate a child's birthday cake, or put a few in cellophane bags as party favours.

Marbled cookie pops

Preparation time: 30 minutes (+ 30 minutes chilling time)
Cooking time: 15 minutes (per batch)
Makes: 30

180 g (6¼ oz) unsalted butter, just softened
220 g (7¾ oz/1 cup) caster (superfine) sugar
1 teaspoon vanilla extract
1 egg, at room temperature
few drops of red food colouring
50 g (1¾ oz) dark chocolate, melted
1 tablespoon unsweetened cocoa powder
2 teaspoons milk
300 g (10½ oz/2 cups) plain (all-purpose) flour
¾ teaspoon baking powder
30 paddle pop sticks, coloured, if desired (see page 120)

TIP: Keep pops in an airtight container in a cool place for up to 1 week.

1 Use an electric mixer to beat the butter and sugar in a small bowl until pale and creamy. Add the vanilla and egg and beat until well combined. Divide the mixture evenly among three separate bowls.

2 Tint one bowl of mixture with the red food colouring to desired colour. Stir the melted chocolate, cocoa and milk into another bowl. Leave one plain. Sift 100 g (3½ oz/⅔ cup) of the flour and ¼ teaspoon baking powder into each bowl. Use a flat-bladed knife to mix each to a soft dough. Divide each dough in half and roll each into a 40 cm (16 in) log. Twist all six logs together into a log about 6 cm (2½ in) in diameter, creating a marbled effect. Cut the log in half, wrap in non-stick baking paper to keep its shape and place on a tray. Refrigerate for 30 minutes or until firm.

3 Preheat oven to 180°C (350°F/Gas 4). Line three large baking trays with non-stick baking paper.

4 Use a sharp knife to trim the edges of the logs and cut into 1 cm (½ in) thick slices. Insert a stick halfway into each biscuit and place 3 cm (1¼ in) apart on the lined trays. Gently roll each biscuit with a rolling pin or gently press with the palm of your hand to reshape. Bake for 15 minutes, in batches if necessary, swapping the trays halfway through cooking, or until lightly golden and cooked through. Allow to cool for 5 minutes on trays before transferring to a wire rack to cool completely.

Butterfly pops

Preparation time: 20 minutes (+ 30 minutes chilling and 2 hours standing time)
Cooking time: 13–15 minutes
Decorating time: 30 minutes
Makes: 12

1 quantity vanilla or chocolate biscuit dough (page 116)
2 quantities royal icing (see page 124)
food colouring of your choice
cachous, to decorate
liquorice strips, to decorate
12 lollipop sticks

TIP: Keep pops in an airtight container in a cool place for up to 3 days.

1 Preheat oven to 160°C (315°F/Gas 2–3). Line two large baking trays with non-stick baking paper.

2 Divide the biscuit dough into two even portions. Roll out each portion evenly between two sheets of non-stick baking paper until 6 mm (¼ in) thick. Place the dough on the baking trays and refrigerate for 30 minutes or until firm.

3 Cut the dough into 12 shapes using a 7.5 cm (3 in) wide butterfly-shaped cutter and place 2 cm (¾ in) apart on the lined trays. Reroll and cut any scraps of dough if necessary. Bake for 13–15 minutes, swapping the trays halfway through cooking, or until lightly golden and cooked through. Allow to cool for 5 minutes on trays before transferring to a wire rack to cool completely.

4 To decorate, reserve one quantity of the royal icing for white details. Divide the remaining quantity of icing evenly among three bowls and tint each using food colouring to desired colours. Cover all the bowls with plastic wrap until ready to use. Working with one colour at a time, use a small palette knife that has been dipped in hot water to spread the icing to thickly coat the butterflies.

5 Use a piping (icing) bag fitted with a 2 mm (¹⁄₁₆ in) round nozzle to pipe a thin line of white icing around each butterfly then pipe a thicker line in the centre of the wings to resemble an abdomen. Pipe dots over the wings and place a cachous on each dot to decorate. Cut the liquorice into 3 cm (1¼ in) strips and press into the icing at the top of each butterfly to resemble antennae, applying a little more icing if necessary to help them stick.

6 Use some of the remaining icing to attach a lollipop stick to the back of each biscuit. Place on a wire rack for 2 hours or until the icing sets and the sticks are firmly attached.

Cake pops

Double choc cake pops

Preparation time: 30 minutes (+ 1 hour chilling time)
Cooking time: nil
Decorating time: 40 minutes
Makes: 25

½ chocolate buttercake (see page 119)
½ quantity chocolate buttercream (see page 123)
300 g (10½ oz) white chocolate, chopped
30 x 15 cm (6 in) thin wooden skewers
250 g (9 oz) dark chocolate, chopped

TIP: Keep pops in an airtight container in the fridge for up to 2 days. Stand at room temperature for 20 minutes before serving.

1 Line a tray with non-stick baking paper. Break the buttercake into rough pieces. Use your hands to rub the cake pieces over a large bowl to form small, even crumbs. Add the buttercream and mix well until evenly combined. Squeeze 1 tablespoonful of the cake mixture firmly so that it holds together and then roll it into a 3 cm (1¼ in) ball. Place on the lined tray. Repeat with the remaining mixture to make 25 balls in total. Refrigerate for 30 minutes or until firm.

2 Put the white chocolate in a heatproof bowl over a saucepan of simmering water, making sure the base of the bowl doesn't touch the water. Stir until the chocolate melts. Dip the end of a skewer into the melted chocolate to coat about 2 cm (¾ in), then insert into a cake ball and return to the lined tray. Repeat with the remaining sticks, melted chocolate and cake balls. Refrigerate for 10 minutes or until the sticks are secure. Reserve the remaining melted chocolate.

3 To decorate, dip the pops one at a time into the reserved melted chocolate and gently tap the skewer on the edge of the bowl to remove excess chocolate, gradually turning as you go to create an even coating. (You may need to gently reheat the chocolate by placing the bowl over a saucepan of simmering water if it becomes too thick for coating.) Insert the sticks into a polystyrene block or similar to keep them upright. Refrigerate the pops for 10 minutes or until the chocolate sets. Reserve the remaining white chocolate.

4 Put the dark chocolate in a heatproof bowl over a saucepan of simmering water, making sure the base of the bowl doesn't touch the water. Stir until the chocolate melts. Repeat the coating process with the pops and the dark chocolate, inserting the sticks back into the polystyrene. Refrigerate the pops for 10 minutes or until the chocolate sets.

5 Drizzle with the reserved white chocolate as desired, to decorate.

Christmas pudding pops

Preparation time: 30 minutes (+ 1 hour 30 minutes chilling time)
Cooking time: nil
Decorating time: 25 minutes
Makes: 24

350 g (12 oz) bought Christmas (fruit) cake
½ quantity vanilla buttercream (see page 123),
   made with 2 teaspoons brandy or dark rum
100 g (3½ oz) bought marzipan
red and green food colouring
1 quantity royal icing (see page 124)
24 lollipop sticks

1 Line a tray with non-stick baking paper. Break the fruit cake into rough pieces. Use your hands to rub the cake pieces over a large bowl to form small crumbs. Add the buttercream and mix well until evenly combined. Squeeze 1 heaped tablespoonful of the mixture firmly so it holds together and then roll it into a 4 cm (1½ in) ball. Place on the lined tray. Repeat with the remaining mixture to make 24 balls in total. Refrigerate for 1 hour or until firm.

2 Divide the marzipan in half. Tint one half with the red food colouring to desired colour. Tint the remaining half of the marzipan with the green food colouring to desired colour. Roll the red marzipan into 5 mm (¼ in) balls. Take small portions of the green marzipan and shape into small leaves (alternatively, roll out the green marzipan and use a 2 cm (¾ in) leaf cutter to cut out the leaves).

3 To decorate, spoon ½ teaspoonful of the royal icing on top of each cake ball, allowing it to thickly run down the sides and partially coat the balls (if the icing is too thick, add a little water). Return the balls to the lined tray. Decorate each with three marzipan balls and two leaves. Return to the fridge for 30 minutes or until firm.

4 Insert the lollipop sticks through the base of the puddings to serve.

TIP: Keep pops in an airtight container in the fridge for up to 5 days.

Milk chocolate cake pops

Preparation time: 30 minutes (+ 1 hour chilling time)
Cooking time: 15 minutes
Decorating time: 20 minutes
Makes: 24

75 g (2¾ oz) unsalted butter
75 g (2¾ oz) milk chocolate, chopped
75 g (2¾ oz/⅓ cup, firmly packed) brown sugar
2 eggs, lightly whisked, at room temperature
75 g (2¾ oz/½ cup) self-raising flour, sifted
24 short, thick wooden skewers
50 g (1¾ oz) milk chocolate, melted
1 quantity milk chocolate ganache (see page 124),
   cooled to coating consistency
silver cachous, to decorate

TIPS: Keep pops in an airtight container in a cool place for up to 2 days.

You can also use greased metal mini muffin tins instead of the silicone moulds. Cook the cakes for 12 minutes. They may be a little harder to remove from the tin so use a small palette knife to ease them out.

1 Preheat oven to 160°C (315°F/Gas 2–3). Place two 12-hole 25 ml (1 fl oz) capacity silicone mini muffin moulds on two baking trays (see tip).

2 Combine the butter and chopped chocolate in a heatproof bowl over a saucepan of simmering water, making sure the base of the bowl doesn't touch the water. Stir until melted. Remove from the heat, add the brown sugar and egg and mix with a wooden spoon until combined. Stir in the flour until just combined. Spoon the mixture into the muffin holes, dividing evenly.

3 Bake for 15 minutes or until cooked when tested with a skewer. Set aside to cool for 15 minutes. Carefully remove the cakes from the moulds then transfer to a wire rack to cool completely.

4 Line a tray with non-stick baking paper. Dip the end of a skewer into the melted chocolate to coat about 2 cm (¾ in), then insert into the top of a cake and place on the lined tray. Repeat with the remaining skewers, melted chocolate and cakes. Refrigerate for 30 minutes or until the skewers are secure.

5 To decorate, dip the pops one at a time into the ganache to cover half of the cake and gently tap the skewer on the edge of the bowl to remove excess ganache. (You may need to gently reheat the ganache in a heatproof bowl over a saucepan of simmering water if it becomes too thick for coating.) Sprinkle the tops with the cachous then insert the sticks into a polystyrene block or similar to keep them upright. Refrigerate the pops for 30 minutes or until the ganache sets.

Red velvet cake pops

Preparation time: 30 minutes (+ 50 minutes chilling time)
Cooking time: nil
Decorating time: 40 minutes
Makes: 46

> 1 red velvet cake (see page 119)
> 1 quantity vanilla buttercream (see page 123)
> 600 g (1 lb 5 oz) white chocolate
> 46 red or white lollipop sticks

1 Line a tray with non-stick baking paper. Break the velvet cake into rough pieces. Use your hands to rub the cake pieces over a large bowl to form small, even crumbs. Remove 60 g (2¼ oz/¾ cup) of the cake crumbs and set aside. Add the buttercream to the remaining cake crumbs and mix well until evenly combined. Squeeze 1 tablespoonful of the cake mixture firmly so that it holds together and then roll it into a 3 cm (1¼ in) ball. Place on the lined tray. Repeat with the remaining mixture to make 46 balls in total. Refrigerate for 30 minutes or until firm.

2 Put the chocolate in a medium heatproof bowl over a saucepan of simmering water, making sure the base of the bowl doesn't touch the water. Stir until the chocolate melts. Dip the end of a lollipop stick into the melted chocolate to coat about 2 cm (¾ in), then insert into a cake ball and return to the lined tray. Repeat with the remaining sticks, melted chocolate and cake balls. Refrigerate for 10 minutes or until the sticks are secure. Reserve the remaining melted chocolate.

3 To decorate, dip the pops one at a time into the remaining chocolate and gently tap the lollipop stick on the edge of the bowl to remove excess chocolate, turning as you go to create an even coating. (You may need to gently reheat the chocolate over a saucepan of simmering water if it is too thick for coating.) Sprinkle with the reserved cake crumbs then insert the sticks into a polystyrene block or similar to keep them upright. Refrigerate the pops for 10 minutes or until the chocolate sets.

TIPS: Keep pops in an airtight container in the fridge for up to 2 days. Stand at room temperature for 30 minutes before serving.

These can be used to decorate wedding, anniversary or birthday cakes: bake a large round red velvet cake, ice with vanilla or chocolate buttercream and decorate with the pops.

This recipe can be halved and the remaining cake half can be frozen for another time.

Mini lamington pops

Preparation time: 10 minutes (+ 30 minutes standing time)
Cooking time: nil
Decorating time: 30 minutes
Makes: 40

1 slab buttercake (see pages 119–120)
270 g (9½ oz/3 cups) desiccated coconut
2 quantities chocolate glacé icing (see page 120),
    made with an extra 60 ml (2 fl oz/¼ cup) water
40 small wooden skewers or lollipop sticks

1 Use a serrated knife to level the top of the cake if necessary. Trim the crusts from the sides. Cut the cake into 40 x 3 cm (1¼ in) squares.
2 Place 90 g (3¼ oz/1 cup) of the coconut on a sheet of non-stick baking paper. Use two forks to dip a piece of the cake in the glacé icing. Holding the cake on top of the fork, tap it gently on the side of the bowl to remove any excess icing. (Add a little more boiling water if the icing becomes too thick for coating.) Roll the cake in the coconut, then place on a wire rack. Repeat with the remaining cake squares, icing and coconut, adding extra coconut for rolling as needed. Insert the skewers into the pops and set aside at room temperature for 30 minutes or until the icing sets.

TIPS: Keep pops in an airtight container in a cool place for up to 2 days.

It is best to make the buttercake the day before as it will be easier to cut and won't crumble as much.

This recipe can be halved and the remaining cake half can be frozen for another time.

Carrot cake pops

Preparation time: 30 minutes (+ 50 minutes chilling time)
Cooking time: nil
Decorating time: 20 minutes
Makes: 50

1 carrot cake (see page 119)
1 quantity vanilla buttercream
   (see page 123)
2 tablespoons finely grated lemon zest
600 g (1 lb 5 oz) white chocolate
150 g (5½ oz) walnut pieces, lightly
   toasted, finely chopped
50 lollipop sticks or 10 cm (4 in) wooden
   skewers

TIP: Keep pops in an airtight container in the fridge for up to 2 days. Stand at room temperature for about 15 minutes before serving.

1 Line a tray with non-stick baking paper. Break the cake into rough pieces. Use your hands to rub the cake pieces over a large bowl to form small, even crumbs. Combine the buttercream and lemon zest, add to the cake crumbs and mix well until evenly combined. Squeeze 1 tablespoonful of the mixture firmly so it holds together and then roll it into a 3 cm (1¼ in) ball. Place on the lined tray. Repeat with the remaining mixture to make 50 balls in total. Refrigerate for 30 minutes or until firm.

2 Put the chocolate in a heatproof bowl over a saucepan of simmering water, making sure the base of the bowl doesn't touch the water. Stir until the chocolate melts. Dip the end of a lollipop stick into the melted chocolate to coat about 2 cm (¾ in), then insert into a cake ball and return to the lined tray. Repeat with the remaining sticks, melted chocolate and cake balls. Refrigerate for 10 minutes or until the sticks are secure. Reserve the remaining melted chocolate.

3 To decorate, dip the pops one at a time into the melted chocolate and gently tap the lollipop stick on the edge of the bowl to remove excess chocolate, gradually turning as you go to create an even coating. (You may need to gently reheat the chocolate by placing the bowl over a saucepan of simmering water if it becomes too thick for coating.) Sprinkle with the walnuts then insert the sticks into a polystyrene block or similar to keep them upright. Refrigerate the pops for 10 minutes or until the chocolate sets.

Lime & coconut cake pops

Preparation time: 30 minutes (+ 50 minutes chilling time)
Cooking time: nil
Decorating time: 25 minutes
Makes: 25

½ buttercake (see page 119)
½ quantity lime buttercream (see page 123)
400 g (14 oz) white chocolate
25 lollipop sticks
55 g (2 oz/¾ cup) shredded coconut

1 Line a tray with non-stick baking paper. Break the buttercake into rough pieces. Use your hands to rub the cake pieces over a large bowl to form small, even crumbs. Add the buttercream and mix well until evenly combined. Squeeze 1 tablespoonful of the mixture firmly so that it holds together and then roll it into a 3 cm (1¼ in) ball. Place on the lined tray. Repeat with the remaining mixture to make 25 balls in total. Refrigerate for 30 minutes or until firm.

2 Put the chocolate in a heatproof bowl over a saucepan of simmering water, making sure the base of the bowl doesn't touch the water. Stir until the chocolate melts. Dip the end of a lollipop stick into the melted chocolate to coat about 2 cm (¾ in), then insert into a cake ball and return to the lined tray. Repeat with the remaining sticks, melted chocolate and cake balls. Refrigerate for 10 minutes or until the sticks are secure. Reserve the remaining melted chocolate.

3 To decorate, spread the shredded coconut on a plate. Dip the pops one at a time into the remaining melted chocolate and gently tap the lollipop stick on the edge of the bowl to remove excess chocolate, gradually turning as you go to create an even coating. (You may need to gently reheat the chocolate by placing the bowl over a saucepan of simmering water if it becomes too thick for coating.) Sprinkle with the shredded coconut then insert the sticks into a polystyrene block or similar to keep them upright. Refrigerate the pops for 10 minutes or until the chocolate sets.

TIP: Keep pops in an airtight container in the fridge for up to 2 days. Stand at room temperature for about 15 minutes before serving.

Petit four cake pops

Preparation time: 20 minutes (+ 1 hour chilling time)
Cooking time: nil
Decorating time: 40 minutes
Makes: 30

¼ buttercake (see page 119)
¼ quantity vanilla buttercream (see page 123)
1 teaspoon finely grated orange zest
400 g (14 oz) white chocolate
30 lollipop sticks
food colouring and sprinkles of your choice

TIP: Keep pops in an airtight container in the fridge for up to 2 days. Stand at room temperature for 30 minutes before serving.

1 Line a tray with non-stick baking paper. Break the buttercake into rough pieces and then use your hands to rub the pieces together over a large bowl to form small, even crumbs. Combine the buttercream and orange zest, add to the cake crumbs and mix well until evenly combined. Squeeze 2 teaspoonfuls of the cake mixture firmly so that it holds together and then roll it into a 2 cm (¾ in) ball. Place on the lined tray. Repeat with the remaining mixture to make 30 balls in total. Refrigerate for 30 minutes or until firm.

2 Put 250 g (9 oz) of the chocolate in a heatproof bowl over a saucepan of simmering water, making sure the base of the bowl doesn't touch the water. Stir until the chocolate melts. Dip the end of a lollipop stick into the melted chocolate to coat about 2 cm (¾ in), then insert into a cake ball and return to the lined tray. Repeat with the remaining sticks, melted chocolate and cake balls. Refrigerate for 10 minutes or until the sticks are secure. Reserve the remaining melted chocolate.

3 To decorate, dip the pops one at a time into the reserved melted chocolate and gently tap the lollipop stick on the edge of the bowl to remove excess chocolate, gradually turning as you go to create an even coating. (You may need to gently reheat the chocolate by placing the bowl over a saucepan of simmering water if it becomes too thick for coating.) Insert the sticks into a polystyrene block or similar to keep them upright. Refrigerate the pops for 10 minutes or until the chocolate sets.

4 Put the remaining chocolate in a heatproof bowl over a saucepan of simmering water, making sure the base of the bowl doesn't touch the water. Stir until the chocolate melts. Tint the chocolate with the food colouring to the desired colour. Dip the top of the pops in the coloured melted chocolate, sprinkle with the sprinkles and insert the sticks back into the polystyrene block. Refrigerate for 10 minutes or until the chocolate sets.

Brownie pops

Preparation time: 20 minutes (+ 15 minutes standing
  and 2 hours 15 minutes chilling time)
Cooking time: 15 minutes
Decorating time: 25 minutes
Makes: 24

TIPS: Keep pops in an
airtight container in the
fridge for up to 3 days. Stand
at room temperature for
15-30 minutes before serving.

You can also use greased
metal mini muffin tins instead
of the silicone moulds. Cook
the brownies for 12 minutes.
They may be a little harder
to remove from the tin so
use a small palette knife to
ease them out.

  125 g (4½ oz) butter, just softened
  165 g (5¾ oz/¾ cup) caster (superfine) sugar
  ½ teaspoon vanilla extract
  2 eggs, at room temperature
  100 g (3½ oz/⅔ cup) plain (all-purpose) flour
  40 g (1½ oz/⅓ cup) unsweetened cocoa powder
  150 g (5½ oz) dark chocolate (70% cocoa solids)
  24 lollipop sticks
  1 quantity milk chocolate ganache (see page 124),
    cooled to coating consistency

1 Preheat oven to 160°C (315°F/Gas 2–3). Place two 12-hole 25 ml (1 fl oz) capacity silicone mini muffin moulds on two baking trays (see tip).

2 Use an electric mixer to beat the butter, sugar and vanilla in a medium bowl, scraping down the side as necessary, until pale and creamy. Add the eggs one at a time, beating well after each addition. Sift the flour and cocoa together. Add to the butter mixture and beat on low speed until just combined.

3 Spoon the mixture into the muffin holes, dividing evenly. Bake for 15 minutes or until cooked when tested with a skewer. Stand the brownies in the moulds for 15 minutes to cool. Carefully remove the brownies from the moulds and transfer to a wire rack. Refrigerate for 1 hour or until firm.

4 Line a tray with non-stick baking paper. Shave one-third of the dark chocolate with a sharp knife or vegetable peeler. Chop the remaining chocolate and put in a heatproof bowl over a saucepan of simmering water, making sure the base of the bowl doesn't touch the water. Stir until the chocolate melts. Dip the end of a lollipop stick into the melted chocolate to coat about 2 cm (¾ in), then insert into the base of a brownie and place on the lined tray. Repeat with the remaining sticks, melted chocolate and brownies. Refrigerate for 15 minutes or until the sticks are secure.

5 To decorate, dip the pops one at a time into the chocolate ganache and gently tap the lollipop stick on the edge of the bowl to remove excess ganache, gradually turning as you go to create an even coating. (You may need to gently reheat the ganache in a heatproof bowl over a saucepan of simmering water if it becomes too thick for coating.) Sprinkle the tops with the shaved chocolate then insert into a polystyrene block or similar to keep them upright. Refrigerate for 1 hour or until the ganache sets.

Mint chocolate cake pops

Preparation time: 20 minutes (+ 1 hour chilling time)
Cooking time: nil
Decorating time: 20 minutes
Makes: 25

½ chocolate buttercake (see page 119)
½ quantity chocolate buttercream (see page 123)
1 teaspoon mint essence, or to taste
300 g (10½ oz) dark chocolate
25 lollipop sticks
green sprinkles, to decorate

1 Line a tray with non-stick baking paper. Break the buttercake into rough pieces. Use your hands to rub the pieces over a large bowl to form small, even crumbs. Combine the buttercream and mint and mix well. Add to the cake crumbs and mix well until evenly combined. Squeeze 1 tablespoonful of the cake mixture firmly so that it holds together and then roll it into a 3 cm (1¼ in) ball. Place on the lined tray. Repeat with the remaining mixture to make 25 balls in total. Refrigerate for 30 minutes or until firm.
2 Put the chocolate in a heatproof bowl over a saucepan of simmering water, making sure the base of the bowl doesn't touch the water. Stir until the chocolate melts. Dip the end of a lollipop stick into the melted chocolate to coat about 2 cm (¾ in), then insert into a cake ball and return to the lined tray. Repeat with the remaining sticks, melted chocolate and cake balls. Refrigerate for 10 minutes or until the sticks are secure. Reserve the remaining melted chocolate.
3 To decorate, dip the pops one at a time into the reserved melted chocolate and gently tap the lollipop stick on the edge of the bowl to remove excess chocolate, gradually turning as you go to create an even coating. (You may need to gently reheat the chocolate over a saucepan of simmering water if it becomes too thick for coating.) Sprinkle with the sprinkles to coat evenly then insert the sticks into a polystyrene block or similar to keep them upright. Refrigerate the pops for 20 minutes or until the chocolate sets.

TIPS: Keep pops in an airtight container in the fridge for up to 2 days. Stand at room temperature for about 15 minutes before serving.

We covered our lollipop sticks with straws: simply cut straws to the same length as the lollipop sticks, slide them over the sticks and press gently into the pops to secure.

Cheesecake pops

Preparation time: 25 minutes (+ 2 hours 40 minutes chilling time)
Cooking time: nil
Makes: 12

150 g (5½ oz) bought plain sweet butter biscuits,
   broken into large chunks
250 g (9 oz) cream cheese
30 g (1 oz/¼ cup) icing (confectioners') sugar
1 tablespoon freshly squeezed lemon juice
1 teaspoon vanilla essence
50 g (1¾ oz) white chocolate, melted
12 lollipop sticks

1 Put the biscuits in a food processor and process until
fine crumbs form. Transfer to a medium bowl.
2 Put the cream cheese, icing sugar, lemon juice and vanilla
in the food processor and process until smooth and well
combined. Add half the biscuit crumbs and use the pulse
button to process until just combined. Transfer to a bowl,
cover and refrigerate for 2 hours or until firm.
3 Line a tray with non-stick baking paper. Spread the
remaining biscuit crumbs on a plate. Roll a tablespoonful of
the mixture into a 3 cm (1¼ in) ball and then roll in the biscuit
crumbs to coat. Dip the end of a lollipop stick into the melted
chocolate to coat about 2 cm (¾ in) and then insert into the
centre of the ball. Place on the lined tray. Repeat with the
remaining cream cheese mixture, biscuit crumbs, sticks and
chocolate.
4 Refrigerate the pops for 40 minutes or until well chilled.

TIP: Keep pops in an airtight container in the fridge for up to 2 days. Serve straight from the fridge.

Chocolate cake pops

Preparation time: 20 minutes (+ 1 hour chilling time)
Cooking time: nil
Decorating time: 25 minutes
Makes: 16

½ chocolate buttercake (see page 119)
½ quantity chocolate buttercream (see page 123)
300 g (10½ oz) dark chocolate, chopped
100's & 1000's, to decorate
16 lollipop sticks

1 Line a tray with non-stick baking paper. Break the buttercake into rough pieces. Use your hands to rub the cake pieces together over a large bowl to form small, even crumbs. Add the buttercream and mix well until evenly combined. Squeeze 1 heaped tablespoonful of the cake mixture firmly so that it holds together and then roll it into a 4 cm (1½ in) ball. Place on the lined tray. Repeat with the remaining mixture to make 16 balls in total. Refrigerate for 30 minutes or until firm.

2 Put the chocolate in a heatproof bowl over a saucepan of simmering water, making sure the base of the bowl doesn't touch the water. Stir until the chocolate melts. Dip the end of a lollipop stick into the melted chocolate to coat about 2 cm (¾ in), then insert into a cake ball and return to the lined tray. Repeat with the remaining sticks, melted chocolate and cake balls. Refrigerate for 10 minutes or until the sticks are secure. Reserve the remaining melted chocolate.

3 To decorate, dip the pops one at a time into the reserved melted chocolate and gently tap the lollipop stick on the edge of the bowl to remove excess chocolate, gradually turning as you go to create an even coating. (You may need to gently reheat the chocolate by placing the bowl over a saucepan of simmering water if it becomes too thick for coating.) Sprinkle with 100's & 1000's to coat then insert the sticks into a polystyrene block or similar to keep them upright. Refrigerate the pops for 20 minutes or until the chocolate sets.

TIPS: Keep pops in an airtight container in the fridge for up to 2 days. Stand at room temperature for 15 minutes before serving.

Serve these instead of a birthday cake for a child's birthday. Use a cylindrical-shaped piece of polystyrene, which can be painted and then decorated with ribbon. Insert the pops into the foam.

To decorate our lollipop sticks, we wrapped them in coloured adhesive tape.

Party time

Fishy pops

Preparation time: 15 minutes (+ 30 minutes chilling and 2 hours standing time)
Cooking time: 15 minutes
Decorating time: 40 minutes
Makes: 12

1 quantity vanilla biscuit dough (see page 116)
12 milk chocolate buttons
2 quantities royal icing (see page 124)
12 brown mini M&M's
12 jelly snakes (various colours)

food colouring of your choice
12 pink mini marshmallows
12 paddle pop sticks, coloured,
if desired (see page 120)

1 Preheat oven to 180°C (350°F/Gas 4). Line two large baking trays with non-stick baking paper.
2 Divide the biscuit dough into two even portions. Roll out each portion evenly between two sheets of non-stick baking paper until 7 mm (⅜ in) thick. Place the dough on the baking trays and refrigerate for 30 minutes or until firm.
3 Cut the dough into 12 rounds using a 7 cm (2¾ in) cutter and 12 rounds using a 4.5 cm (1¾ in) cutter.
4 Position the 7 cm rounds on the trays, leaving 8 cm (3¼ in) between each. Place a 4.5 cm round next to each 7 cm round (this will become a tail). Use a 2.5 cm (1 in) round cutter to cut a half moon from the 4.5 cm rounds to make the tail. Secure join of tail and body with ½ teaspoon of the remaining dough, pressing gently together.
5 Bake the biscuits for 15 minutes, swapping the trays around after 10 minutes, or until lightly golden and cooked through. Allow to cool for 5 minutes on trays before transferring to a wire rack to cool completely.
6 Meanwhile, to decorate, place the chocolate buttons top-side down on a chopping board. Use a piping (icing) bag fitted with a 2 mm (1/16 in) plain nozzle to pipe a round of the royal icing onto each chocolate button and attach an M&M to each to make an eye. Set aside for 30 minutes or until set.
7 Use scissors dipped in a little icing sugar to cut a snake into 1 mm (1/32 in) pieces. Divide the remaining icing among three bowls and tint each one with the food colouring to desired colours. Spread a fish biscuit with desired colour. Position the snake pieces on the icing to make scales.
8 Use scissors dipped in a little icing sugar to cut a mini marshmallow in half three-quarters of the way through and attach to the fish as lips. Attach the eyes with a little icing. Use a fork to make lines on the tail to make fins. Repeat with the remaining biscuits, icing, lollies and eyes.
9 Use some of the icing to attach a paddle pop stick to the back of each biscuit. Set aside for 2 hours or until the icing sets and the sticks are firmly attached.

Rocky road pops

Preparation time: 20 minutes (+ 5–10 minutes standing and 15 minutes chilling time)
Cooking time: nil
Makes: 32

250 g (9 oz/3 cups) mixed pink and white marshmallows, halved
160 g (5¾ oz) roughly chopped unsalted peanuts
100 g (3½ oz/½ cup) glacé (candied) cherries, halved
65 g (2½ oz/1 cup) shredded coconut
350 g (12 oz) dark chocolate, chopped
32 short wooden skewers

1 Line the base and sides of a 20 cm (8 in) square cake tin with two overlapping strips of non-stick baking paper.
2 Combine the marshmallows, peanuts, cherries and coconut in a large bowl. Place the chocolate in a small heatproof bowl over a saucepan of simmering water, making sure the base of the bowl doesn't touch the water. Stir until the chocolate melts. Remove from the heat and allow to stand for 5–10 minutes or until cooled slightly. Add the chocolate to the marshmallow mixture and mix well.
3 Spoon the mixture into the tin and use the back of a spoon to press evenly over the base. Refrigerate for 15 minutes or until set.
4 Carefully lift the rocky road out of the tin, peeling away the paper. On a board, cut into 32 5 x 2.5 cm (2 x 1 in) pieces and insert a skewer halfway into each piece.

TIP: Keep pops in an airtight container in the fridge for up to 1 week.

White chocolate cluster pops

Preparation time: 25 minutes (+ 10–15 minutes chilling time)
Cooking time: 18 minutes
Makes: 15

15 lollipop sticks
155 g (5½ oz/1 cup) unsalted macadamia nuts,
  coarsely chopped
250 g (9 oz) white chocolate, chopped
105 g (4¼ oz/⅔ cup) finely chopped dried apricots
55 g (2 oz/⅓ cup) currants

1 Preheat oven to 180°C (350°F/Gas 4). Line two baking trays
with non-stick baking paper. Place the lollipop sticks about
5 cm (2 in) apart on the trays.
2 Spread the nuts on another baking tray and cook for
8 minutes or until lightly toasted and aromatic, shaking
the tray once or twice to ensure even toasting.
3 Put the chocolate in a small heatproof bowl over a saucepan
of simmering water, making sure the base of the bowl doesn't
touch the water. Stir until the chocolate melts. Remove the
bowl from the saucepan and stir in three-quarters of the nuts
and dried fruit.
4 Spoon a tablespoonful of the chocolate mixture onto the
end of a lollipop stick on the tray and spread to a 5 cm (2 in)
round. Repeat with the remaining sticks and chocolate mixture.
Sprinkle with the remaining nuts and fruit. Refrigerate for
10–15 minutes or until set.

TIP: Keep pops in an
airtight container in the
fridge for up to 1 week.

Farmyard cookie pops

Preparation time: 20 minutes (+ 30 minutes chilling time,
  cooling time and 2 hours standing time)
Cooking time: 12–15 minutes
Decorating time: 1 hour
Makes: 24

1 quantity vanilla biscuit dough (see page 116)
2 quantities royal icing (see page 124)
yellow food colouring
24 rainbow choc chips
30 g (1 oz/⅓ cup) desiccated coconut
8 pink cachous
64 white mini marshmallows
24 paddle pop sticks, coloured,
  if desired (see page 120)

TIPS: For these pops we used 7 cm (2¾ in) sheep, 8.5 cm (3¼ in) rabbit and 7 cm (2¾ in) duck (all measured lengthways) biscuit cutters.

Use these to decorate a child's birthday cake iced with green buttercream and sprinkled with green-tinted shredded coconut. Serve the remaining biscuits on the side.

1 Preheat oven to 180°C (350°F/Gas 4). Line two baking trays with non-stick baking paper.
2 Divide the biscuit dough into two even portions. Roll out each portion evenly between two sheets of non-stick baking paper until 5 mm (¼ in) thick. Place the dough on the baking trays and refrigerate for 30 minutes or until firm.
3 Cut the dough into 24 animal shapes using biscuit cutters (see tip) and place 2 cm (¾ in) apart on the lined trays. Reroll and cut any scraps of dough if necessary.
4 Bake for 12–15 minutes, swapping the trays after 7 minutes, or until lightly golden and cooked through. Allow to cool on trays for 5 minutes before transferring to a wire rack to cool completely.
5 To decorate, place ⅓ cup of the royal icing in a bowl, cover with plastic wrap and set aside. Divide the remaining royal icing evenly among three small bowls. Tint one portion of the icing to desired colour using the yellow food colouring. Use a small palette knife that has been dipped in hot water to spread the yellow icing over the duck biscuits, leaving the beak and feet bare. Stand for 5 minutes or until almost set. Use a fork to make lines on the duck to show the wing and tail. Attach a rainbow choc chip as an eye. Spread one portion of the white icing over the rabbit biscuits to coat and sprinkle with the coconut. Attach the cachous as a nose and red rainbow chocolate chips as eyes. Use scissors to cut each marshmallow into four pieces horizontally. Spread the remaining white icing over the sheep biscuits, leaving the head and legs bare. Position the marshmallows on the body of the sheep. (It is better to work from the base of the body to the top.) Attach a rainbow choc chip with a little icing as an eye.
6 Use the reserved white icing to attach a paddle pop stick to the back of each biscuit. Set aside on a lined tray, decorated side up, for 2 hours or until the icing sets and the sticks are firmly attached.

Rum & raisin cluster pops

Preparation time: 25 minutes (+ 4 hours or overnight soaking
  and 15 minutes chilling time)
Cooking time: 5 minutes
Makes: 32

> 100 g (3½ oz/¾ cup) raisins
> 1 tablespoon Malibu (coconut and rum liqueur)
> 50 g (1¾ oz/⅔ cup) shredded coconut
> 400 g (14 oz) dark chocolate, chopped
> 100 g (3½ oz/⅔ cup) pine nuts, toasted
> 32 lollipop sticks
> flaked or shredded coconut, extra, to decorate

1 Combine the raisins and Malibu in a small bowl, cover
and leave to soak for 4 hours or overnight.
2 Preheat the oven to 150°C (300°F/Gas 2). Spread the 50 g
shredded coconut on a baking tray and bake for 5 minutes
or until lightly golden. Remove from the oven, lift the baking
paper and coconut off the tray and set aside to cool. Line the
tray with non-stick baking paper.
3 Place the chocolate in a small heatproof bowl over a
saucepan of simmering water, making sure the base of
the bowl doesn't touch the water. Stir occasionally until
just melted and smooth. Remove from the heat.
4 Drain the raisins well, add to the melted chocolate with
the coconut and pine nuts and stir well. Use an oiled teaspoon
to place a heaped spoonful of the mixture on the tray, on top
of a lollipop stick. Repeat with the remaining mixture and
sticks. Sprinkle with the extra coconut. Refrigerate for
15 minutes or until set.

TIP: Keep pops in an
airtight container in the
fridge for up to 1 week.

White chocolate fudge pops

Preparation time: 20 minutes (+ 1 hour 30 minutes chilling
  and 30 minutes standing time)
Cooking time: nil
Makes: 30

100 g (3½ oz) unsalted butter, chopped
480 g (1 lb 1 oz) white chocolate, chopped
1 egg, lightly whisked
2 teaspoons vanilla extract
250 g (9 oz) bought plain sweet biscuits, broken
150 g (5½ oz) dried apricots, chopped
90 g (3¼ oz/1⅓ cups) shredded coconut
orange food colouring
30 lollipop sticks

TIP: Keep pops in an airtight container in the fridge for up to 2 days. Stand at room temperature for 30 minutes before serving.

1 Combine the butter and 180 g (6¼ oz) of the chocolate in a small heatproof bowl over a saucepan over simmering water, making sure the base of the bowl doesn't touch the water. Stir until melted and smooth. Add the egg and vanilla and stir well to combine. Set aside.

2 Meanwhile, put the biscuits in a food processor and process until fine crumbs form. Transfer to a large bowl. Place the apricots in the processor bowl and process until finely chopped. Add to the biscuits with the chocolate mixture and use your hands to mix well until evenly combined. If the mixture is soft, cover and refrigerate for 1 hour or until firm enough to roll into balls.

3 Line a tray with non-stick baking paper. Roll tablespoonfuls of the mixture into balls and place on the lined tray. Refrigerate for 30 minutes or until firm.

4 To decorate, place the coconut in a small zip-lock bag, add a few drops of the orange food colouring and rub until tinted to desired colour. Spread on a plate.

5 Put the remaining white chocolate in a small bowl over a saucepan of simmering water, making sure the base of the bowl doesn't touch the water. Stir until the chocolate melts. Remove from the heat. Working with one pop at a time, insert a lollipop stick and then dip the pop into the melted chocolate and gently tap the lollipop stick on the edge of the bowl to remove excess chocolate, gradually turning as you go to create an even coating. (You may need to gently reheat the chocolate by placing the bowl over a saucepan of simmering water if it becomes too thick for coating.) Gently roll in the coconut to coat lightly then insert the stick into a polystyrene block or similar to keep them upright. Set the pops aside for 30 minutes or until the chocolate sets.

Robot pops

Preparation time: 30 minutes (+ 3 hours or overnight standing time)
Cooking time: nil
Decorating time: 20 minutes
Makes: 12

> 1 x 132 g (4½ oz) pack puffed rice cereal bars (6 bars)
> cornflour (cornstarch), to dust
> 500 g (1 lb 2 oz) bought fondant icing, tinted
>   with your choice of food colouring
> 12 wooden sticks
> whisked egg white, for brushing
> assorted lollies (such as Lifesavers, coloured
>   musk sticks, raspberry liquorice rope and
>   mixed sugar-coated jubes), to decorate

1 Line a large tray with non-stick baking paper. Cut each rice cereal bar in half widthways.

2 Lightly dust a bench with cornflour. Use a rolling pin lightly dusted with cornflour to roll out the fondant icing to a 5 mm (¼ in) thick square. Use a sharp knife to cut the icing into twelve 14 x 6 cm (5½ x 2½ in) rectangles. Cover the icing with plastic wrap to prevent it from drying out. Take a piece of icing and wrap it neatly around a rice cereal bar, pressing the ends together on the sides and base to enclose the bar. Place on the lined tray. Repeat with the remaining icing and rice cereal bars. Push a stick into each bar.

3 To decorate, brush the underside of each lolly with a little egg white to moisten and press lightly onto the icing to create the robot faces, necks and antennas. Set aside for 3 hours or overnight for the icing to harden and the lollies to stick.

TIP: Keep pops in an airtight container in a cool place for up to 2 days.

Sweetheart pops

Preparation time: 20 minutes (+ 30 minutes chilling time, cooling time and 2 hours standing time)
Cooking time: 15 minutes
Decorating time: 30 minutes
Makes: 14

TIPS: Keep pops in an airtight container in a cool place for up to 4 days.

Wrap a few of these in cellophane with ribbon and attach to a gift for a loved one.

1 quantity vanilla biscuit dough (see page 116)
1 quantity glacé icing (see page 120)
pink food colouring
red food colouring
200 g (7 oz) white chocolate, melted
14 flat wooden skewers or paddle pop sticks

1 Preheat oven to 180°C (350°F/Gas 4). Line two large baking trays with non-stick baking paper.

2 Divide the biscuit dough into two even portions. Roll out each portion evenly between two sheets of non-stick baking paper until 5 mm (¼ in) thick. Place the dough on the baking trays and refrigerate for 30 minutes or until firm.

3 Cut the dough into 28 shapes using a 6 cm (2½ in) heart cutter and place 2 cm (¾ in) apart on the lined trays. Reroll and cut any scraps of dough if necessary.

4 Bake the biscuits for 15 minutes, swapping the trays halfway through cooking, or until lightly golden and cooked through. Allow to cool on trays for 5 minutes before transferring to a wire rack to cool completely.

5 To decorate, divide the glacé icing evenly between two bowls. Use the food colouring to tint both portions to desired colour. Cover the bowls so the icing doesn't dry out. Spoon 1 teaspoon of the icing onto the top of a biscuit and use a palette knife that has been dipped in hot water to spread the icing carefully to the edges of the biscuit. Repeat with the remaining icing and half the biscuits, colouring half the biscuits in each colour. (You should have 14 iced biscuits and 14 plain biscuits.) You may need to add 1–2 teaspoons of boiling water to the icing if it becomes too thick.

6 Spread 1 teaspoon of the melted chocolate evenly onto the underside of a plain biscuit. Position a skewer into the centre of the biscuit over the chocolate and spread with another teaspoon of chocolate. Sandwich with an iced biscuit. Repeat with the remaining biscuits, chocolate and sticks. Set aside for 2 hours or until the chocolate sets and the sticks are firmly attached.

Caramel popcorn pops

Preparation time: 15 minutes (+ 10 minutes standing time)
Cooking time: 10–15 minutes
Makes: 8

40 g (1½ oz/3½ cups) plain popcorn
160 g (5¾ oz) unsalted roasted peanuts
  (see tip), coarsely chopped
440 g (15½ oz/2 cups) caster (superfine) sugar
80 ml (2½ fl oz/⅓ cup) water
20 g (¾ oz/1 tablespoon) unsalted butter
8 x 26 cm (10½ in) butcher's skewers

1 Combine the popcorn and peanuts in a large bowl. Combine the sugar and water in a small saucepan and stir over low heat until the sugar dissolves. Bring to the boil and cook over medium–high heat, without stirring, for about 8 minutes or until the mixture turns a golden caramel colour, brushing down the side of the pan with a pastry brush dipped in water occasionally.

2 Working quickly and carefully (the mixture will spit and be very hot), remove the pan from the heat, add the butter and swirl to combine. Pour the mixture over the popcorn and peanuts and stir with a wooden spoon until all the nuts and popcorn are evenly coated.

3 Cool the mixture for about 2–3 minutes or until cool enough to handle with rubber gloves on (the mixture should still be quite hot and too hot to touch without the gloves). Put on thick rubber gloves and, working quickly, shape an eighth of the mixture around the blunt end of each skewer (about 10 cm/4 in long and 3.5 cm/1½ wide), pressing firmly so the mixture sticks. Push each skewer into a polystyrene block or similar to keep them upright. Set aside for 10 minutes or until the caramel sets.

TIPS: These pops are best served on the day of making. However, they can be kept in an airtight container in a cool place for up to 2 days (they may go slightly sticky on storing).

You can use salted roasted peanuts for a salty caramel flavour.

It is important to work quickly when pressing the popcorn mixture onto the skewers as the caramel sets very quickly, making it difficult to shape.

Sports ball pops

Preparation time: 20 minutes (+ 30 minutes chilling time,
  cooling time and 2 hours 30 minutes standing time)
Cooking time: 15–18 minutes
Decorating time: 25 minutes
Makes: 12

1 quantity vanilla biscuit dough (see page 116)
2 quantities royal icing (see page 124)
black, green, yellow, orange and red food colouring
30 g (1 oz/⅓ cup) desiccated coconut
orange sprinkles, to decorate
12 paddle pop sticks

TIPS: Keep pops in an airtight container in a cool place for up to 4 days.

These pops are perfect for a kid's party or wrapped in cellophane and attached to a present to decorate.

1 Preheat oven to 160°C (315°F/Gas 2–3). Line two baking trays with non-stick baking paper.
2 Divide biscuit dough into two portions. Roll out each evenly between two sheets of non-stick baking paper until 7 mm (⅜ in) thick. Place on the baking trays. Refrigerate for 30 minutes.
3 Cut the dough into 12 rounds using an 8 cm (3¼ in) cutter and place 2 cm (¾ in) apart on the lined trays. Reroll and cut any scraps of dough if necessary.
4 Bake the biscuits for 15–18 minutes, swapping the trays halfway through cooking, or until lightly golden and cooked through. Stand on trays for 5 minutes; transfer to a wire rack to cool completely.
5 To decorate, place ¼ cup of the icing in a piping (icing) bag fitted with a 2 mm (¹⁄₁₆ in) round nozzle. Tint ¼ cup of the royal icing black and place in a piping (icing) bag fitted with a 2 mm round nozzle. Cover the ends of both piping nozzles with a damp cloth so the icing doesn't dry out. Divide the remaining icing into four equal portions and place in separate bowls. Tint one icing portion lime green using the green and yellow food colouring; one portion orange; and one portion red. Leave the remaining portion white. Cover all the bowls with plastic wrap.
6 To make the tennis balls, place the coconut and a few drops of green and yellow colouring in a small zip-lock bag and rub until the coconut is evenly coloured. Spread four of the biscuits with the lime icing and then sprinkle with the coconut. Set aside for 10 minutes or until the icing is firm. Tip off excess coconut. Use the white icing in the piping (icing) bag to pipe lines on the tennis balls as shown.
7 To make the basketballs, spread four of the biscuits with the orange icing then sprinkle with the orange sprinkles. Set aside for 10 minutes or until the icing is firm. Tip off excess sprinkles. Use the black icing in the piping (icing) bag to pipe lines on the basketballs as shown.
8 To make the cricket balls, spread four of the biscuits with the red icing. Set aside for 10 minutes or until the icing is firm. Use the white icing in the piping (icing) bag to pipe lines on cricket balls as shown.
9 Use the remaining white icing to attach a paddle pop stick to the back of each biscuit. Set aside for 2 hours or until the icing sets and the sticks are firmly attached.

Giant freckle pops

Preparation time: 20 minutes (+ 1 hour standing time)
Cooking time: nil
Makes: 12

600 g (1 lb 5 oz) compound milk chocolate
sprinkles of your choice (such as 100's & 1000's,
   silver or mixed cachous and/or coloured sprinkles)
12 paddle pop sticks

1 Line two large trays with non-stick baking paper.
2 Put the chocolate in a medium heatproof bowl over a saucepan of simmering water, making sure the base of the bowl doesn't touch the water. Stir until the chocolate melts.
3 Spoon 12 rounds of the melted chocolate onto the lined trays, about 12 cm (4½ in) apart, and place a paddle pop stick into each with the top in the centre of the chocolate. Tap the trays on the bench until the chocolate forms circles about 8 cm (3¼ in) wide and covers the sticks. Sprinkle the chocolate discs with sprinkles of your choice. Set aside at room temperature for 1 hour or until the chocolate sets and the sticks are firmly attached.

TIP: Keep pops in an airtight container in the fridge for up to 1 week.

Brown sugar & cinnamon Christmas tree pops

Preparation time: 20 minutes (+ 30 minutes chilling time)
Cooking time: 20 minutes
Decorating time: 10 minutes
Makes: 24

1 quantity brown sugar & cinnamon biscuit dough (see page 116)
1 quantity royal icing (see page 124)
24 paddle pop sticks
silver cachous or small coloured lollies, to decorate

1 Preheat oven to 160°C (315°F/Gas 2–3). Line two baking trays with non-stick baking paper.

2 Divide the biscuit dough into two even portions. Roll out each portion evenly between two sheets of non-stick baking paper until 8 mm (⅜ in) thick. Place the dough on the baking trays and refrigerate for 30 minutes or until firm.

3 Cut the dough into 24 shapes using a 10 cm long x 5 cm wide (4 in x 2 in) Christmas tree cutter and place 3 cm (1¼ in) apart on the lined trays. Reroll and cut any scraps of dough if necessary.

4 Bake the biscuits for 20 minutes, swapping the trays halfway through cooking, or until lightly golden and cooked through. Cool on trays for 5 minutes then transfer to a wire rack to cool completely.

5 Use some of the royal icing to attach a paddle pop stick to the back of each biscuit.

6 Place the remaining icing in a piping (icing) bag fitted with a 2 mm (¹⁄₁₆ in) plain nozzle. (Alternatively, use a zip-lock bag with a small hole cut in the corner.) Pipe the icing in a zig-zag pattern over the cooled biscuits and sprinkle with the cachous or lollies. Set aside for 2 hours or until the icing sets and the sticks are firmly attached.

TIPS: Keep pops in an airtight container in a cool place for up to 3 days.

These cookie pops are perfect to attach name tags to and use as place cards for your Christmas celebrations.

Pecan pie pops

Preparation time: 30 minutes (+ 30 minutes chilling time)
Cooking time: 25 minutes
Makes: 15

1 quantity vanilla biscuit dough (see page 116)
15 paddle pop sticks
1 egg, lightly whisked
2 tablespoons coffee crystals

Pecan filling
1 tablespoon milk
2 tablespoons cornflour (cornstarch)
65 g (2½ oz) unsalted butter
110 g (3¾ oz/½ cup, firmly packed) brown sugar
60 ml (2 fl oz/¼ cup) sweetened condensed milk
100 g (3½ oz/1 cup) whole pecans, chopped

TIP: Keep pops in an airtight container in a cool place for up to 2 days.

1 To make the pecan filling, place the milk and cornflour in a small heavy-based saucepan and mix until a smooth paste forms. Add the butter, brown sugar and condensed milk and stir over medium heat until the mixture boils. Reduce heat to low and cook, stirring, for 5 minutes or until slightly thickened. Stir in the pecans and set aside to cool. Cover and refrigerate until needed.
2 Preheat oven to 180°C (350°F/Gas 4). Line two large baking trays with non-stick baking paper.
3 Divide the biscuit dough into two even portions. Roll out each portion evenly between two sheets of non-stick baking paper until 5 mm (¼ in) thick. Place the dough on the baking trays and refrigerate for 30 minutes or until firm.
4 Cut the dough into 30 shapes using a 6 cm (2½ in) flower shape or round cutter. Reroll and cut any scraps of dough if necessary. Place half of the rounds on the lined trays about 2 cm (¾ in) apart and place a paddle pop stick on each round, extending into the centre of the pastry (about one-third of the stick is inserted in the pie). Spoon a heaped teaspoon of the pecan mixture into the centre of the pastry rounds on the trays. Brush the edges lightly with the whisked egg and then top each with another round of dough. Pinch the edges together to seal. Brush the tops of the pies with a little more egg and then sprinkle with the coffee crystals.
5 Bake the biscuits for 16–18 minutes, swapping the trays after 8 minutes, or until lightly golden and cooked through. Allow to cool on trays for 5 minutes before transferring to a wire rack to cool completely.

Easter bunny cookie pops

Preparation time: 20 minutes (+ 30 minutes chilling time, cooling time and 2 hours standing time)
Cooking time: 13–15 minutes
Decorating time: 25 minutes
Makes: 14

    1 quantity vanilla biscuit dough (see page 116)
    2 quantities glacé icing (see page 120)
    food colouring of your choice
    silver cachous, to decorate
    14 paddle pop sticks

1 Preheat oven to 160°C (315°F/Gas 2–3). Line two baking trays with non-stick baking paper.

2 Divide the biscuit dough into two even portions. Roll out each portion evenly between two sheets of non-stick baking paper until 7 mm (3/8 in) thick. Place the dough on the baking trays and refrigerate for 30 minutes or until firm.

3 Cut the dough into 14 shapes using a 12.5 cm (4½ in) long rabbit cutter and place 2 cm (¾ in) apart on the lined trays. Reroll and cut any scraps of dough if necessary.

4 Bake the biscuits for 13–15 minutes, swapping the trays after 8 minutes, or until lightly golden and cooked through. Cool on trays.

5 To decorate, use the food colouring to tint the glacé icing as desired. Use a small palette knife that has been dipped in hot water to spread the icing over the biscuits. Decorate each bunny with a cachous for an eye. Use some of the icing to attach a paddle pop stick to the back of each biscuit. Set aside for 2 hours or until the icing sets and the sticks are firmly attached.

TIPS: Keep pops in an airtight container in a cool place for up to 2 days.

Use lengths of ribbon to tie around the neck of each rabbit to decorate and give as an Easter present, if desired.

Gingerbread houses

Preparation time: 25 minutes (+ 30 minutes chilling and 2 hours standing time)
Cooking time: 10–12 minutes
Decorating time: 45 minutes
Makes: 16

100 g (3½ oz) butter, just softened
110 g (3¾ oz/½ cup, firmly packed)
  brown sugar
2 teaspoons ground ginger
1 teaspoon ground cinnamon
1 egg, at room temperature
1 teaspoon vanilla essence
60 ml (2 fl oz/¼ cup) golden syrup
225 g (8 oz/1½ cups) self-raising flour
75 g (2¾ oz/½ cup) plain (all-purpose) flour
1 quantity royal icing (see page 124)

16 lollipop or paddle pop sticks
4 natural ice cream wafers
32 mini red jelly beans
32 red heart-shaped lollies

TIP: Keep pops in an airtight container in a cool place for up to 5 days.

1 Preheat oven to 180°C (350°F/Gas 4). Line two baking trays with non-stick baking paper.

2 Use an electric mixer to beat the butter, sugar, ginger and cinnamon in a medium bowl until pale and creamy. Add the egg and vanilla and beat until well combined. Beat in the golden syrup. Add the flours and mix until well combined.

3 Turn the dough out onto a lightly floured bench and knead lightly until smooth. Divide the dough into two portions. Roll each portion between two pieces of non-stick baking paper until 5 mm (¼ in) thick. Refrigerate for 30 minutes or until firm.

4 Cut the dough into 32 shapes using a 6 cm (2½ in) house-shaped cutter and place 2 cm (¾ in) apart on the lined trays. Reroll and cut any scraps of dough if necessary. Bake the biscuits for 10–12 minutes, swapping the trays halfway through cooking, or until lightly golden and cooked through. Allow to cool for 5 minutes on trays before transferring to a wire rack to cool completely.

5 To decorate, place a biscuit top-side down on the bench. Spread half a teaspoon of the royal icing in the centre of the biscuit and position a paddle pop stick on top, extending into the centre of the biscuit. Top with a little more icing and then sandwich with another biscuit. Repeat with the remaining biscuits, some of the remaining icing and the sticks.

6 Cut the wafers into 32 x 5 x 2 cm (2 x ¾ in) rectangles (or to fit tops of houses as roofs). Spread each piece with a little of the remaining icing and position onto a gingerbread house to make a roof. Use a piping (icing) bag fitted with a 2 mm (1/16 in) round nozzle to pipe a little of the icing to attach the jelly beans along the ridge of the roof and the heart lollies for the windows. Pipe icing along the house rooflines to look like snow. Set aside for 2 hours or until the icing sets and the sticks are firmly attached.

Pretty party stars

Preparation time: 20 minutes (+ 30 minutes chilling and 2 hours standing time)
Cooking time: 20 minutes
Decorating time: 30 minutes
Makes: 30

1 quantity vanilla biscuit dough (see page 116)
2 quantities glacé icing (see page 120)
food colouring of your choice
30 lollipop sticks (covered with pipe cleaners),
  or paddle pop sticks
cachous and sprinkles of your choice, to decorate

1 Preheat oven to 160°C (315°F/Gas 2–3). Line two large baking trays with non-stick baking paper.

2 Divide the biscuit dough into two even portions. Roll out each portion evenly between two sheets of non-stick baking paper until 7 mm (⅜ in) thick. Place the dough on the baking trays and refrigerate for 30 minutes or until firm.

3 Cut the dough into 30 shapes using a 5 cm (2 in) star cutter and place 2 cm (¾ in) apart on the lined trays.

4 Bake the biscuits for 20 minutes, swapping the trays halfway through cooking, or until lightly golden and cooked through. Allow to cool for 5 minutes on trays before transferring to a wire rack to cool completely.

5 To decorate, divide the glacé icing into two portions and tint each with the food colouring to desired colour. Use a palette knife dipped in hot water to spread the icing over the stars. Sprinkle with the cachous and sprinkles to decorate. Use some of the remaining icing to attach a stick to the back of each biscuit. Set aside at room temperature for 2 hours or until the icing sets and the sticks are firmly attached.

TIP: Keep pops in an airtight container in a cool place for up to 4 days.

Ice cream pops

Preparation time: 10 minutes (+ several hours or overnight freezing time)
Cooking time: nil
Decorating time: 20 minutes
Makes: 12

500 ml (17 fl oz/2 cups) firm vanilla
   ice cream (see tip)
12 paddle pop sticks
300 g (10½ oz) good-quality milk chocolate
   (see tip), chopped
1 tablespoon vegetable oil
dollar sprinkles, 100's & 1000's or other
   coloured sprinkles, to decorate

1 Line two baking trays with non-stick baking paper and place in the freezer until very cold.

2 Working quickly, use a large melon baller to scoop 12 x 3 cm (1¼ in) diameter balls of ice cream onto the chilled lined baking trays. Quickly insert a paddle pop stick into each ball and return the tray to the freezer for several hours or overnight until the ice cream balls are very firm.

3 Put the chocolate in a heatproof bowl over a saucepan of simmering water, making sure the base of the bowl does not touch the water. Stir until the chocolate melts. Stir in the vegetable oil. Remove from the heat and cool to room temperature.

4 Remove one tray of ice cream balls from the freezer and dip, one at a time, into the chocolate to coat and then allow the excess chocolate to drip off. Immediately sprinkle with the sprinkles to coat the tops, then immediately return to the freezer on the tray. Repeat with the remaining ice cream balls, chocolate and sprinkles. Refreeze for 2 hours or overnight. Serve straight from the freezer.

TIPS: Keep pops in an airtight container in the freezer for up to 1 week.

A firm ice cream rather than a very light and airy variety is easier to work with.

Use good-quality chocolate as cheaper brands may not adhere well to the ice cream.

You can use melted dark or white chocolate to coat the balls, or decorate with lightly toasted flaked almonds or flaked chocolate instead of the sprinkles.

Snowflake cookie pops

Preparation time: 20 minutes (+ 30 minutes chilling
   and 2 hours standing time)
Cooking time: 12–15 minutes
Decorating time: 40 minutes
Makes: 20

> 1 quantity vanilla biscuit dough (see page 116)
> 2 quantities royal icing (see page 124)
> silver cachous, to decorate
> sanding sugar (see tip) (optional), to decorate
> 24 flat wooden or paddle pop sticks

1 Preheat oven to 180°C (350°F/Gas 4). Line two baking
trays with non-stick baking paper.
2 Divide the biscuit dough into two even portions. Roll out
each portion evenly between two sheets of non-stick baking
paper until 5 mm (¼ in) thick. Place the dough on the baking
trays and refrigerate for 30 minutes or until firm.
3 Cut the dough into 20 shapes using 6–8 cm (2½–3¼ in)
snowflake cutters and place 2 cm (¾ in) apart on the lined
trays. Reroll and cut any scraps of dough if necessary.
4 Bake the biscuits for 12–15 minutes, swapping the trays
after 7 minutes, or until lightly golden and cooked through.
Allow to cool for 5 minutes on trays before transferring to a
wire rack to cool completely.
5 To decorate, use a palette knife that has been dipped
in hot water to spread the royal icing over half the biscuits
(reserving about ⅓ cup of the icing to attach the sticks). Use
a piping (icing) bag fitted with a 1 mm (1/32 in) plain nozzle to
pipe desired designs onto both the iced and uniced biscuits.
Decorate with the cachous and sprinkle with the sanding sugar,
if using. Use some of the reserved icing to attach a stick to the
back of each biscuit. Set aside for 2 hours or until the icing sets
and the sticks are firmly attached.

TIPS: Keep pops in an
airtight container in a cool
place for up to 4 days.

Sanding sugar is a
speciality decorating
sugar. The crystals are
coarser than regular
granulated sugar, which
gives it its 'sparkling'
appearance. It is
available in white or
coloured shades from
speciality cake-decorating
shops. You can use
regular granulated
sugar instead.

Halloween pops

Preparation time: 25 minutes (+ 30 minutes chilling
  and 2 hours standing time)
Cooking time: 15 minutes
Decorating time: 25 minutes
Makes: 16

TIPS: Keep pops in an
airtight container in a cool
place for up to 2 days.

To achieve strong black and
orange colours for these
pops, use colour pastes
instead of liquid colours.

    1 quantity chocolate biscuit dough (see page 116)
    2 quantities royal icing (see page 124)
    black and orange food colouring paste (see tip)
    2 x 16 cm (6¼ in) piece liquorice strap
    16 round mini liquorice allsorts
    16 paddle pop sticks, coloured, if desired (see page 120)

1 Preheat oven to 160°C (315°F/Gas 2–3). Line two baking trays with non-stick baking paper.
2 Divide the biscuit dough into two even portions. Roll out each portion evenly between two
sheets of non-stick baking paper until 7 mm (⅜ in) thick. Place the dough on the baking trays
and refrigerate for 30 minutes or until firm.
3 Cut the dough into 16 rounds using an 8 cm (3¼ in) cutter and place 2 cm (¾ in) apart on the
lined trays. Reroll and cut any scraps of dough if necessary.
4 Bake the biscuits for 15 minutes, swapping the trays halfway through cooking, or until lightly
golden and cooked through. Allow to cool for 5 minutes on trays before transferring to a wire
rack to cool completely.
5 Use the black food colouring to tint ⅓ cup of the royal icing to desired colour and place in
a piping (icing) bag fitted with a 2 mm (1/16 in) round nozzle. Cover the tip of the nozzle with a
damp cloth. Place the remaining icing in a bowl and tint with the orange food colouring to desired
colour. Cover the bowl with plastic wrap.
6 To decorate, use a small palette knife that has been dipped in hot water to spread the orange
icing over a cooled biscuit to coat. Use the black icing in the piping (icing) bag to pipe a spiral
over the orange icing. Use a skewer to draw 8–10 separate lines from the centre of the spiral to
the outside edge to make a spider's web. Repeat with the remaining biscuits, the orange and the
black icing.
7 To make the spiders, cut 8 x 3 cm (1¼ in) pieces from the liquorice strap. Cut each piece in half
lengthwise. Make three cuts at each end of each piece without cutting all the way through to
form eight legs and place one set of legs on each of the spider's webs. Use the black icing in the
piping (icing) bag to pipe a small round of icing in the centre of the legs and then place a liquorice
allsort over the icing. Use some of the remaining icing to attach a paddle pop stick to the back of
each biscuit. Set aside for 2 hours or until the icing sets and the sticks are firmly attached.

Flower garden pops

Preparation time: 20 minutes (+ 30 minutes chilling time
and 2 hours 45 minutes standing time)
Cooking time: 10–12 minutes
Decorating time: 30 minutes
Makes: 12

TIPS: Keep pops in an
airtight container in a cool
place for up to 2 days.

To make the tinted
coconut, place the coconut
in a small zip-lock bag and
add green food colouring
gradually, rubbing until
coconut is evenly coloured.

½ quantity vanilla biscuit dough (see page 116)
2 quantities royal icing (see page 124)
green, yellow and pink food colouring
pink sprinkles
12 green pipe cleaners
12 small paddle pop sticks
12 chocolate buttercake cupcakes (see pages 119–120), baked in brown paper cases
65 g (2½ oz) green-tinted shredded coconut (see tip)

1 Preheat oven to 180°C (350°F/Gas 4). Line two baking trays with non-stick baking paper.

2 Roll out the dough evenly between two sheets of non-stick baking paper until 5 mm (¼ in) thick.
Place the dough on one of the baking trays and refrigerate for 30 minutes or until firm.

3 Cut the dough into 24 shapes using a 5 cm (2 in) flower cutter and place 2 cm (¾ in) apart
on the lined trays. Reroll and cut any scraps of dough if necessary.

4 Bake the biscuits for 10–12 minutes, swapping the trays after 7 minutes, or until lightly golden
and cooked through. Stand for 5 minutes on trays then transfer to a wire rack to cool completely.

5 To decorate, tint half of the royal icing with green food colouring. Cover and set aside. Tint ¼ cup of
the remaining royal icing with yellow food colouring. Tint the remaining icing with pink food colouring.
Reserve ⅓ cup pink icing. Use a small palette knife to spread the remaining pink icing over the biscuits
to coat. Sprinkle with the pink sprinkles. Set the biscuits aside for 30 minutes or until the icing sets.

6 Twist the pipe cleaners around the paddle pop sticks to form the stem and leaves of flowers,
leaving 1.5 cm (⅝ in) at the top and base of the stick.

7 Spread a little of the reserved pink icing over one side of the end of a decorated paddle pop
stick. Press the icing side of the stick onto the underside of a biscuit to attach. Top the stick with
a little more icing and then sandwich with another of the flower biscuits. Repeat with the remaining
icing, decorated sticks and biscuits. Set aside for 2 hours or until the sticks are firmly attached.

8 Use a piping (icing) bag fitted with a 2 mm (¹⁄₁₆ in) round nozzle to pipe the yellow icing to
make centres of flowers. (Alternatively, use a zip-lock bag with a small hole cut in the corner.)
Set aside for 15 minutes or until the icing sets.

9 Spread the cupcakes with the green icing then sprinkle with the green-tinted coconut to
resemble grass. Stick a flower into the top of each cupcake.

Fast & simple

Marshmallow pops

Preparation time: 15 minutes (+ 15 minutes chilling time)
Cooking time: nil
Decorating time: 10 minutes
Makes: 50

50 lollipop sticks
300 g (10½ oz) white chocolate, melted
50 large pink and white marshmallows
   (about 1 x 250 g/9 oz packet)
sprinkles of your choice, to decorate

1 Line a baking tray with non-stick baking paper. Dip the end
of a lollipop stick into the melted chocolate to coat about 2 cm
(¾ in) of the end, then insert into the base of a marshmallow
and place on the lined tray. Repeat with the remaining sticks,
chocolate and marshmallows. Place in the freezer for 5 minutes
or until the sticks are secure. Reserve the remaining melted
chocolate.

2 To decorate, dip the marshmallows into the reserved melted
chocolate to coat the top half and then press and roll the top
into the sprinkles. Insert the sticks into a polystyrene block or
similar to keep them upright. Refrigerate for 10 minutes or
until the chocolate sets.

TIPS: Keep pops in an
airtight container in a cool
place for up to 1 week.

These are a fun kids'
activity at a birthday
party. Have the children
decorate their own pops
before devouring them!

Strawberry pops

Preparation time: 15 minutes (+ 30 minutes standing time)
Cooking time: nil
Makes: 24

24 strawberries (about 2 x 250 g/9 oz punnets)
24 lollipop sticks
200 g (7 oz) white chocolate, melted
200 g (7 oz) dark chocolate, melted

1 Line a baking tray with non-stick baking paper. Thread each strawberry onto a lollipop stick.
2 Dip half the strawberries in the melted white chocolate, coating the bottom half, and allow the excess chocolate to drip off. Place on the lined tray. Repeat with the remaining strawberries and melted dark chocolate. Set aside in a cool place for 30 minutes or until the chocolate sets.

TIPS: Keep pops in a cool place (not the fridge as they will sweat). They are best eaten within 24 hours of making.

These are great served with coffee at wedding or birthday celebrations.

Black & white pops

Preparation time: 10 minutes (+ 2 hours 30 minutes standing time)
Cooking time: nil
Decorating time: 45 minutes
Makes: 24

24 sandwiched chocolate biscuits
24 thin or flat wooden skewers
2 quantities royal icing (see page 124)
black food colouring paste

1 Push each biscuit onto a skewer through the soft centre, taking care not to dislodge the biscuits on either side.
2 To decorate, divide the icing between two bowls and tint one portion using the black food colouring. Cover the bowls with plastic wrap so the icing doesn't dry out. Use a small paintbrush to thickly coat one side of each biscuit with the black icing and then coat the other side with the white icing. Insert the sticks into a polystyrene block or similar to keep them upright. Set the biscuits aside for 30 minutes or until the icing sets. Cover the remaining icing well so it does not dry out.
3 Divide the remaining icing between two piping (icing) bags fitted with 2 mm (1/16 in) plain piping nozzles. Pipe a thin outline around each biscuit in the opposite colour to the base (white on black, black on white) then decorate the centre of each with spots or stripes. Insert the pops back into the polystyrene as they are finished. Set aside for 2 hours or until the icing sets.

TIP: Keep pops in an airtight container in a cool place for up to 1 week.

Toffee pear pops

Preparation time: 15 minutes (+ 30 minutes standing time)
Cooking time: 15 minutes
Makes: 16

16 miniature pears or apples
200 g (7 oz) bought marzipan
16 butcher's skewers
440 g (15½ oz/2 cups) caster (superfine) sugar
80 ml (2½ fl oz/⅓ cup) water
¼ teaspoon red food colouring
16 x 5 cm (2 in) paper cases (optional)

1 Line a baking tray with non-stick baking paper. Use a small, sharp knife to remove the pear or apple cores, working from the base of the fruit, leaving a generous cavity. Fill each cavity with marzipan then dry the fruit well with paper towel if necessary. Push a skewer into the top of each pear at a slight angle and at least halfway in.

2 Combine the sugar and water in a small saucepan and stir over low heat until the sugar dissolves. Bring to the boil and cook over medium–high heat, without stirring, for 8–10 minutes or until the mixture turns a golden caramel colour, brushing down the side of the pan with a pastry brush dipped in water occasionally.

3 Working quickly and carefully (the mixture will spit and be very hot), remove the pan from the heat and add the food colouring, swirling to combine well. Holding the pan at an angle so the caramel is deep, and working with one pear at a time, dip each pear in the hot caramel to coat well, allowing the excess caramel to drain off. Place the pears, base down, on the lined tray. Set aside for 30 minutes or until the caramel sets.

4 Place the pears in the paper cases to serve, if using.

TIPS: These pops are best eaten on the day of making.

You can also use 8 small corella pears in place of the miniature pears.

Easy chocolate orange fudge pops

Preparation time: 15 minutes (+ 2 hours chilling time)
Cooking time: 5 minutes
Decorating time: 5 minutes
Makes: 36

395 g (14 oz) sweetened condensed milk
50 g (1¾ oz) unsalted butter, cubed
200 g (7 oz) orange-flavoured dark chocolate,
   finely chopped
200 g (7 oz) dark chocolate, finely chopped
100's & 1000's or coloured sprinkles, to decorate
36 lollipop sticks

TIP: Keep pops in an airtight container in the fridge for up to 2 weeks.

1 Line the base and sides of an 18 cm (7 inch) square cake tin with two overlapping strips of non-stick baking paper.

2 Stir the condensed milk and butter in a saucepan over low heat until the butter melts and the mixture is smooth. Bring just to a simmer, stirring frequently. Remove from the heat, add the chocolate and stir until the chocolate is just melted.

3 Quickly pour the fudge into the lined tin and spread with a palette knife. Refrigerate for 2 hours or until firm.

4 To decorate, remove the fudge from the tin and cut into 3 cm (1¼ in) squares.
Put the 100's & 1000's or sprinkles in a small bowl and roll each piece of fudge to cover. Insert a lollipop stick into the base of each piece of fudge.

Honeycomb & chocolate pops

Preparation time: 20 minutes (+ 1 hour 15 minutes chilling time)
Cooking time: nil
Decorating time: 30 minutes
Makes: 35

200 g (7 oz) bought plain sweet biscuits
300 g (10½ oz) chocolate-covered honeycomb
1 quantity milk chocolate ganache (see page 124),
  cooled to room temperature
600 g (1 lb 5 oz) dark chocolate (70% cocoa
  solids), chopped
35 lollipop sticks

TIP: Serve straight from the fridge within 2 hours of making if possible, as the honeycomb on the outside will start to soften.

1 Line a tray with non-stick baking paper. Place the biscuits in a food processor and pulse until fine crumbs form. Use a sharp knife to finely chop 200 g (7 oz) of the honeycomb on a completely dry chopping board. Stir the biscuit crumbs and honeycomb through the ganache.
2 Roll tablespoons of the mixture into 3 cm (1¼ in) balls and place on the lined tray. Refrigerate for 1 hour or until firm.
3 Put the dark chocolate in a heatproof bowl over a saucepan of simmering water, making sure the base of the bowl doesn't touch the water. Stir until the chocolate is melted. Use a sharp knife to finely chop the remaining honeycomb on a completely dry chopping board.
4 Dip the end of a lollipop stick into the melted dark chocolate to coat about 2 cm (¾ in), then insert into a honeycomb ball and return to the lined tray. Place in the freezer for 2–3 minutes or until the sticks are secure. Reserve the remaining melted chocolate.
5 To decorate, dip the balls one at a time into the reserved melted chocolate and gently tap the lollipop stick on the edge of the bowl to remove excess chocolate, gradually turning as you go to create an even coating. (You may need to gently reheat the chocolate by placing the bowl over a saucepan of simmering water if it becomes too thick for coating.) Sprinkle with the chopped honeycomb then insert the sticks into a polystyrene block or similar to keep them upright. Refrigerate for 10 minutes or until the chocolate sets.

Turkish delight pops

Preparation time: 10 minutes (+ 30 minutes chilling time)
Cooking time: nil
Decorating time: 20 minutes
Makes: 24

300 g (10½ oz) box of Turkish delight
  (about 24 x 2 cm/¾ in square pieces)
24 small sticks
300 g (10½ oz) dark chocolate, chopped
35 g (1¼ oz/¼ cup) very finely chopped pistachios

1 Line a tray with non-stick baking paper. Use a pastry brush to brush off any excess icing sugar from the Turkish delight and insert a stick into each piece at an angle.

2 To decorate, put the dark chocolate in a heatproof bowl over a saucepan of simmering water, making sure the base of the bowl doesn't touch the water. Stir until the chocolate melts. Remove the bowl from the heat and allow to cool. Dip the Turkish delight pops one at a time into the chocolate and gently tap the stick on the edge of the bowl to remove excess chocolate, gradually turning as you go to create an even coating. Place on the lined tray and sprinkle with the pistachios.

3 Refrigerate for 30 minutes or until the chocolate sets.

Fairy floss pops

Preparation time: 20 minutes (+ 30 minutes standing time)
Cooking time: nil
Makes: 12

12 x 5 cm (2 in) bought meringue nests
½ quantity dark chocolate ganache (see page 124),
  chilled until it holds its shape
12 thick 15 cm (6 in) wooden skewers
50 g (1¾ oz) rose-flavoured Iranian fairy floss (pashmak)

1 Place the meringues on a bench. Use two teaspoons or a piping (icing) bag to fill the meringue cavities with the ganache, creating a slight mound. Push the pointed end of a skewer into each nest at a slight angle, avoiding the middle of the base and going into the thicker outer ring. Insert the sticks into a polystyrene block or similar to keep them upright. Set aside at room temperature for 30 minutes or until the ganache is firm.

2 Just before serving, place tufts of the fairy floss on top of each nest (do not put this on any sooner as it will absorb moisture from the ganache and soften quickly). Serve immediately.

Chocolate ball pops

Preparation time: 20 minutes
Cooking time: nil
Makes: 12

12 x 10 cm (4 in) wooden skewers
ribbon
8 Lindt Lindor dark chocolate balls
8 Lindt Lindor milk chocolate balls
8 Lindt Lindor white chocolate balls
12 white chocolate buttons

1 Tie a bow around each skewer with the ribbon.
2 Carefully thread two different chocolate balls onto each skewer. Position a white chocolate button on the end of each skewer as a stand.

TIPS: These pops are easier to assemble if the chocolate balls are at room temperature.

Keep pops in an airtight container in a cool place for up to 1 week.

Basics

Vanilla biscuit dough

Preparation time: 15 minutes
Makes: enough for about 30 x 5–6 cm (2–2½ in) biscuits

335 g (11¾ oz/2¼ cups) plain (all-purpose) flour, sifted
90 g (3¼ oz/¾ cup) icing (confectioners') sugar, sifted
185 g (6½ oz) unsalted butter, chilled, cubed
3 egg yolks
1 teaspoon vanilla essence

1 Combine the flour, icing sugar and butter in the bowl of a food processor and use the pulse button to process until the mixture resembles fine breadcrumbs. Add the egg yolks and vanilla and process using the pulse button until a dough begins to form.
2 Turn the dough out onto a lightly floured surface and knead lightly until smooth. Use as directed.

TIP: Use the dough as directed or keep the dough, divided in half, shaped into a round and wrapped in plastic wrap, in the fridge for up to 1 week. Stand at room temperature for 30 minutes to soften slightly before rolling out.

Variations

Chocolate biscuit dough: Replace 35 g (1¼ oz/¼ cup) of the plain flour with 30 g (1 oz/¼ cup) unsweetened cocoa powder, sifted.
Brown sugar & cinnamon biscuit dough: Replace the icing sugar with 110 g (3¾ oz/½ cup, firmly packed) brown sugar. Combine 2 teaspoons ground cinnamon with the flour, brown sugar and butter before processing.

Attaching sticks to cookie pops

When attaching sticks to cookie pops, royal icing works best because it sets firmly and holds the sticks securely in place. Either spread a little of the icing onto one side of the stick or onto the underside of the biscuit where the stick will be placed, making sure there is enough icing to cover the surface of the stick touching the biscuit. Then press the stick onto the biscuit and lie flat with the biscuit sitting on the stick on either a tray lined with non-stick baking paper or a wire rack for at least 2 hours or until the icing sets and the stick is firmly attached. This step is very important because if you don't allow enough time for the icing to set your pops won't stay on their sticks.

Attaching sticks to cake pops

When attaching sticks to cake pops it is best to coat the end of the stick (usually about 2 cm/¾ in) with melted chocolate before inserting into the pops. Generally, the pops are then chilled until the chocolate sets, firmly attaching the pops to the sticks, before being decorated.

Choosing a stick for your pops

There is a huge range of sticks suitable for pops available from cake-decorating suppliers, kitchenware shops and craft shops. The trick to choosing a suitable stick for your pops is to consider the size and weight of the pops. The larger the pops the shorter the sticks should be in order to hold their weight. Large cookie pops are also best with flatter sticks (such as paddle pop sticks) and large cake pops are best with thicker sticks—both have a greater surface area for attaching to the pop. Also think about the design and type of pop you are making when choosing your sticks—your sticks should complement your pops.

Buttercake

Preparation time: 20 minutes (+ cooling time)
Cooking time: 45–50 minutes
Makes: 1 x 20 cm (8 in) round cake

185 g (6½ oz) unsalted butter, just softened
165 g (5¾ oz/¾ cup) caster (superfine) sugar
2 teaspoons vanilla essence
3 eggs, at room temperature
300 g (10½ oz/2 cups) plain (all-purpose) flour
3 teaspoons baking powder
125 ml (4 fl oz/½ cup) milk

1 Preheat oven to 180°C (350°F/Gas 4). Grease and line a 20 cm (8 in) round cake tin.
2 Use an electric mixer to beat the butter, sugar and vanilla in a medium bowl, scraping down the side as necessary, until pale and creamy. Add the eggs one at a time, beating well after each addition.
3 Sift together the flour and baking powder. On low speed, mix in the flour mixture and milk alternately in two separate batches each until well combined.
4 Spoon the mixture into the prepared tin and use the back of a spoon to smooth the surface. Bake for 45–50 minutes or until a skewer inserted into the centre of the cake comes out clean. Cover with a sheet of baking paper if browning too much towards the end of cooking. Stand in the tin for 5 minutes before turning out onto a wire rack to cool completely. Use as directed.

TIPS: The cake needs to be cooled completely before making into crumbs for cake pops.

Do not allow cake to brown too much or overcook or the pops will be dry.

If cake is used the day it is made it will be moister and softer than cake used 24 hours or more after baking.

The cake can be frozen for up to 1 month. Cut it into quarters (220 g/7¾ oz portions), wrap well in plastic wrap and then seal in an airtight container or freezer bag. Label, date and freeze. Thaw at room temperature before using.

Variations

Chocolate buttercake: Replace 75 g (2¾ oz/½ cup) plain flour with 55 g (2 oz/½ cup) unsweetened cocoa powder, sifted.
Red velvet cake: Sift 1½ tablespoons unsweetened cocoa powder with the flour and baking powder. Add 2 tablespoons red food colouring to the milk before adding it to the cake mixture.
Carrot cake: Add the vanilla with 150 g (5½ oz/1½ cups) finely shredded carrot after the eggs and beat until combined. Sift 1½ teaspoons ground cinnamon and 1½ teaspoons ground nutmeg with the flour and baking powder. Bake for 50 minutes.

Variations (continued)

Cupcakes: Cook the buttercake, chocolate buttercake or red velvet cake in a greased or lined 12-hole 80 ml (2½ fl oz/⅓ cup) capacity muffin tin. Divide the cake mixture among the holes and smooth the surfaces. Bake in an oven preheated to 180°C (350°F/Gas 4) for 18–20 minutes or until a skewer inserted into the centre of a cupcake comes out clean. Stand in the tin for 5 minutes before turning out onto a wire rack to cool completely. Makes 12.

Slab buttercake: Cook the cake mixture in a greased and lined 20 x 30 cm (8 x 12 in) slice tin for 35 minutes.

Glacé icing

Preparation time: 5 minutes
Makes: 125 ml (4 fl oz/½ cup)

> 250 g (9 oz/2 cups) pure icing (confectioners')
> sugar, sifted
> 15 g (½ oz) butter (melted)
> 2½ tablespoons boiling water, approximately

Place the icing sugar in a small heatproof bowl. Add the butter and boiling water and stir with a wooden spoon until the mixture is smooth and has a light coating consistency. Add a little more water, if necessary, to reach desired consistency.

TIP: You may need to sit the bowl of icing in a bowl of hot water or over a saucepan of simmering water and stir regularly to keep the icing at the correct consistency for icing or coating the pops.

Variation

Chocolate glacé icing: Sift 1½ tablespoons cocoa powder with the icing sugar. Increase the boiling water to 60 ml (2 fl oz/¼ cup).

COLOURING YOUR STICKS: Wooden sticks, such as paddle pop sticks and skewers, can be coloured at home to suit your pops. To do this, mix 1 part food colouring of your choice with 2 parts water (the more food colouring you use, the darker the colour will be) in a shallow container. Put the sticks in the container and submerge in the coloured water. Leave for 5-10 minutes then use paper towel to wipe off any excess colouring from the sticks. Leave the sticks to dry on a wire rack before using.

Icings for pops

There are three main icings used in pops making—buttercream, glacé icing and royal icing.
Buttercream is generally used to bind cake crumbs so they can be shaped into cake pops. It also
flavours and sweetens the cake in the same way it would if spread over a cake.

Glacé icing is a simple icing that is smooth and glossy when set. It doesn't set as hard as royal
icing. It is mainly used for decorating.

Royal icing is based on egg whites and pure icing sugar. It becomes very hard when set and for
this reason it is best used when attaching sticks and decorations such as lollies. It can also be used
for decorating as you would glacé icing.

Coating cake and cookie pops with chocolate

Chocolate makes a good coating for cake pops. Different brands and qualities of chocolate will melt to different consistencies, which means you might have to try a few different chocolates before you find the one that gives you the best results. Look for one that will coat the pops evenly, leaving a smooth, even surface. Be careful when you are melting chocolate—if you overheat it, it can become too thick for using as a coating. Either melt your chocolate in a heatproof bowl over a saucepan of barely simmering water (making sure the base of the bowl doesn't touch the water) or in the microwave on a medium setting. White chocolate is more susceptible to overheating than milk or dark chocolate.

Compound chocolates and those that are made specifically for coating without the need for tempering are useful and less temperamental when coating pops. Generally their flavour isn't as superior as good-quality chocolate but they will give your pops a good-looking finish. Chocolate ganache (see page 124) also makes a good coating for pops—it is easy to work with and gives a smooth finish.

Vanilla buttercream

Preparation time: 10 minutes
Makes: 415 g (14¾ oz/2 cups)

> 185 g (6½ oz) unsalted butter, just softened
> 1 teaspoon vanilla extract
> 250 g (9 oz/2 cups) pure icing (confectioners') sugar, sifted

1 Use an electric mixer to beat the butter and vanilla on medium speed until smooth and pale.
2 Reduce the speed to low and add the icing sugar, 60 g (2¼ oz/½ cup) at a time, beating well after each addition until well combined.

Variations

Lime buttercream: Beat in the finely grated zest of 2 limes and 2 teaspoons strained lime juice after the icing sugar.

Chocolate buttercream

Preparation time: 10 minutes
Makes: 375 g (13 oz/1¾ cups)

> 100 g (3½ oz) unsalted butter, just softened
> 1 teaspoon vanilla essence
> 65 g (2½ oz) dark chocolate, melted, cooled
> 185 g (6½ oz/1½ cups) pure icing (confectioners')
>   sugar, sifted
> 2 tablespoons unsweetened cocoa powder

1 Use an electric mixer to beat the butter and vanilla on medium speed until smooth and pale. Beat in the cooled chocolate.
2 Sift together the icing sugar and cocoa powder. Reduce the speed to low and add the icing sugar mixture, 60 g (2¼ oz/½ cup) at a time, beating well after each addition.

TIPS: Do not overbeat the buttercream or let it sit in a warm place for too long as it will become too soft. This will affect the consistency of the cake pop mix, causing the cake pops to lose their shape.

Use the buttercream immediately after making or refrigerate for up to 30 minutes. If chilled for any longer it will be too firm to spread or mix with the cake crumbs for cake pops.

Dark chocolate ganache

Preparation time: 10 minutes (+ 30 minutes chilling time)
Makes: 435 g (15¼ oz/just over 1½ cups)

> 250 g (9 oz) dark chocolate, finely chopped
> 185 ml (6 fl oz/¾ cup) pouring (whipping) cream

1 Place the chocolate in a large heatproof bowl and set aside.

2 Heat the cream in a small saucepan over medium heat until just simmering. Pour over the chocolate and set aside for 2–3 minutes. Stir until the chocolate melts and the mixture is well combined.

3 Use immediately or cover and refrigerate for 30 minutes, stirring often, or until thickened to the desired consistency.

Variation

Milk chocolate ganache: Replace the dark chocolate with milk chocolate.

Royal icing

Preparation time: 10 minutes
Makes: 160 ml (5¼ fl oz/⅔ cup)

> 1 egg white
> 1 teaspoon lemon juice
> 185 g (6½ oz/1½ cup) pure icing
>   (confectioners') sugar, sifted

1 Combine the egg white and lemon juice in a bowl. Use an electric mixer fitted with the whisk attachment to whisk until foamy.

2 With the motor running, add the icing sugar, 60 g (2¼ oz/ ½ cup) at a time, whisking well after each addition. Continue whisking until the mixture forms a smooth and glossy icing that holds its shape.

TIPS: To prevent a crust forming on the top of the icing, cover the surface well with plastic wrap.

Royal icing can be made up to 3 days before using. Cover as above and keep in the fridge. Bring to room temperature before using.

Polystyrene and floral foam

Most decorated pops are best left to set or dry standing up rather than lying down. A block of polystyrene (available from craft shops) or floral foam (available from florists) is a great thing to have on hand for this purpose. The sticks or skewers are easily inserted into the foam, keeping the pops upright and preventing the decorations from being damaged. The foam can be reused again and again so it's worth buying if you plan on making lots of pops. Polystyrene is available from craft shops.

Index

Published in 2011 by Murdoch Books Pty Limited

Murdoch Books Australia
Pier 8/9
23 Hickson Road
Millers Point NSW 2000
Phone: +61 (0) 2 8220 2000
Fax: +61 (0) 2 8220 2558
www.murdochbooks.com.au

Murdoch Books UK Limited
Erico House, 6th Floor
93–99 Upper Richmond Road
Putney, London SW15 2TG
Phone: +44 (0) 20 8785 5995
Fax: +44 (0) 20 8785 5985
www.murdochbooks.co.uk

Publisher: Kylie Walker
Food Development Editor: Anneka Manning
Project Editor: Laura Wilson
Editor: Melissa Penn
Design concept: Alex Frampton and Vivien Valk
Design layout: R.T.J. Klinkhamer
Photographer: Michele Aboud
Stylist: Sarah de Nardi
Illustrator: Alex Frampton
Production: Renee Melbourne

Recipe development: Sonia Greig, Leanne Kitchen, Kirrily La Rosa, Kim Meredith
Food preparation for photography: Grace Campbell

National Library of Australia Cataloguing-in-Publication Data

Title:	Make Me Cake and Cookie Pops
ISBN:	978-1-74266-454-5 (pbk.)
Series:	Make me.
Notes:	Includes index.
Subjects:	Cake, Cookies, Cooking.
Dewey Number:	641.865

A catalogue record for this book is available from the British Library.

Printed by 1010 Printing International Limited, China

OVEN GUIDE: You may find cooking times vary depending on the oven you are using. For fan-forced ovens, as a general rule, set the oven temperature to 20°C (35°F) lower than indicated in the recipe.

On cover: Fishy pops (page 60)